THE CITY OF REFUGE

THE CITY OF REFUGE

GOD'S GRACIOUS PROVISION

FOR HUMANITY'S FAILURES AND

SHORTCOMINGS

HIXFORD N. ALLEN

Copyright © 2023 by Hixford N. Allen.

Library of Congress Control Number:	2023921815
ISBN:	Hardcover	979-8-3694-1146-9
	Softcover	979-8-3694-1147-6
	eBook	979-8-3694-1145-2

All rights reserved. No part of this book may be reproduced or transmitted in any form or by any means, electronic or mechanical, including photocopying, recording, or by any information storage and retrieval system, without permission in writing from the copyright owner.

Scripture quotations unless otherwise indicated are taken from the New King James Version. Copyright 1979, 1980, 1982, 1997 by Thomas Nelson Inc. Used by Permission.

Any people depicted in stock imagery provided by Getty Images are models, and such images are being used for illustrative purposes only.
Certain stock imagery © Getty Images.

Print information available on the last page.

Rev. date: 01/11/2024

To order additional copies of this book, contact:
Xlibris
844-714-8691
www.Xlibris.com
Orders@Xlibris.com
855894

DEDICATION

This book is dedicated to Doreen, my beloved wife and partner in life and ministry. Her love and prayerful support helped to keep me going during the challenging times on this journey. I also dedicate this book to our sons and their wives: Raoul and Tiania, Andre and Ralna, Mark, and Jennifer, and Theophilus and Stacey-Ann; along with our grandkids – Tabitha, Alex, Abigail, Tiffany, Michaela, Nathaniel, Makenzie, Ezekiel, and Nellie. I also hope that those who have failed on their journey of life will find encouragement, hope, and strength to go on.

AUTHOR'S BIOGRAPHY

Bishop Dr. Hixford Allen is the Senior Pastor of the Bronxwood International Church of God in Bronx New York. He was born in Manchester, Jamaica West Indies. He made a personal commitment of his life to the Lord Jesus in June of 1980, and has been faithfully and passionately engaged in Christian service and ministry shortly thereafter. Bishop Allen received his B.A. degree in Theological Studies from the Jamaica Theological Seminary in Kingston, Jamaica; a M.A. degree in Counseling Psychology from the Caribbean Graduate School of Theology, Kingston, Jamaica; and a Doctor of Ministry degree from the Pentecostal Theological Seminary in Cleveland, Tennessee.

Bishop Allen is a credential minister with the Church of God, Cleveland Tennessee, and he has been engaged in pastoral ministry since January 1987 to present. Over the period he has served as lead pastor for four congregations, two in Jamaica West Indies (Duhaney Park New Testament Church of God, and Bethel New Testament Church of God), and two here in the United States (True Life Church of God, Wyandanch, New York, and his present pastorate at Bronxwood International Church of God). While serving as pastor in Jamaica, Bishop Allen also served as guest speaker and bible teacher at the New Testament Church of God yearly youth camps; lecturer and dean at Bethel Bible College, Kingston campus, and as teacher/guidance counselor at Jamaica College high School.

Bishop Allen and his family immigrated to the United States in 1996 and he continued his pastoral ministry at the True Life Church of God. Under Bishop Allen's leadership the True Life Church of God experienced steady growth in just about every area of the church, and the district of churches he supervised grew from four congregations to eight vibrant congregations. The True Life Church of God was instrumental in launching two of those congregations. During his pastoral ministry in New York, Bishop Allen was also privileged to serve as the coordinator/facilitator for the New York State Church of God Pastoral Covenant Group, and member of the New York State Church of God Executive Board. Bishop Allen is a humble and caring servant of the Lord who is highly respected by his peers. His strength lies in his God given ability to preach and teach the word of God; mentor and coach young ministers and prospects for ministry; and provide loving pastoral care to his congregants and to people in general.

Bishop Allen believes in and practices an approach to ministry that is holistic, and which is marked by *liberation, empowerment,* and *transformation* (LET). He believes that those who respond to the gospel are called not only to enjoy the blessings of the gospel, but also to bear the burdens of it. They experience liberation from and its effects, empowered so they can feed themselves and others, and be transformed to the point where they use their God given gifts and abilities to participate in the mission of God to the world (through word and deed) – becoming the embodiment of the gospel - engaging in liberating, empowering, and transforming the lives of others. Bishop Allen also believes that discipleship training should be geared toward people development and not merely toward filling some positions or performing certain tasks.

Bishop Allen's goal for the future is to continue in his pastoral and teaching ministry, with an emphasis on moving the church to become more missional. Broadening our sphere of ministry to help those who have failed in their journey of life due to bad choices to have a chance to recover from their setbacks and be restored to fellowship with God and the community. In his later years, Bishop Allen hopes to transition into a ministry of mentoring young ministers and prospects for ministry.

Bishop Allen and his loving and dedicated wife Doreen have been married for over 44 years, and she has been his partner in ministry over the years. Their union produced four sons: Raoul, Andre, Mark, and Theophilus, who have all contributed to his ministry from their childhood years. Andre and Theophilus both hold ministerial credentials with the Church of God.

BOOK SUMMARY

This book explores the biblical concept of the "City of Refuge" as God's gracious provision for the failures and shortcomings of humanity. We are fallen people living in a fallen world and we need some means of grace to survive. God's mission to redeem and restore fallen humanity through his Son Jesus continues through the church. Various governmental agencies and community outreach organizations have been engaged in helping those who have failed and need special help to recover. The church's mission involves bringing hope to fallen humanity through the proclamation of God's message of redemption and restoration, and by serving as a "city of refuge".

CONTENTS

Acknowledgements..11
Foreword.. 13
Brief Summary of the Text.. 17

Chapter 1   The Case for Building Cities of Refuge 19
Chapter 2   The City of Refuge in Scripture................................. 30
Chapter 3   The City of Refuge – God's Provision for
             Human Weakness 53
Chapter 4   The City of Refuge – God's Provision of
             Grace in Christ... 79
Chapter 5   City of Refuge – The Church as a City of Refuge.... 84
Chapter 6   Recommendations 102

References 109

ACKNOWLEDGEMENTS

I would like to express sincere thanks to the following people who have contributed to the production of this book. To my wife Doreen for her encouragement and prayerful support on the journey; to doctors - Barrington Brown, Samuel Vassell, Isaac Arku, and Sonia Trew-Wisdom for reading the manuscript and providing helpful suggestions and endorsements.

FOREWORD

Reverend Dr. Hixford Allen is a careful, compassionate, and courageous Christian Servant Leader who is a thoughtful scholar. He loves the Lord and loves people and has consequently faithfully served His Lord by serving people as an experienced pastor in God's church. He is particularly gifted with a godly curiosity which is able to recognize and raise critically important practical existential questions. This leads him to seek for credible biblically sound answers in search of understanding, truth and obedience to the will and purpose of God. This book is an expression of this reality which has characterized Dr Allen's life and ministry.

A clear concern of Dr Allen in this book is what may be seen as the unfortunately flawed witness of the Church in respect of its response to its fallen members and ministers to a world that does not recognize God's provision, power, and commitment to rescue and redeem fallen people. Allen contends that the widely established practice of the Church of baring or excluding (sometimes indefinitely) from ministry those who have experienced human failures is not consistent with the revelation of scripture. He contends that this approach provides no opportunity for rescue, support, restoration, and transformation therefore does not bear testimony to the redemptive character of a powerful and loving God.

Dr Allen is at pains to make clear his conviction that sin and wrongdoing have consequences which are rightly and inescapably deserving of punishment. This should be expected by the perpetrator. Allen does not excuse or advocate wrongdoing in this work. He however indicates that he is convinced that intrinsic to the character of God is mercy and grace and that those who represent Him in and to the world, such as the people that comprise the Church, must exemplify these attributes of God, even if they are to be counter cultural in doing so.

The fundamental basis of Dr Allen's theological argument is the Old Testament record of God's provision of the Cities of Refuge and the guiding principles that He instituted to govern how they should function in the life of the community of the people of God. Readers of this book will definitely be enlightened about this issue but not only by the historical information the Cities of Refuge back then but this book will show, with that as a paradigm, it has vital contemporary relevance in understanding complex related issues like; flawed human nature, altitudes and actions that are necessary to facilitate reformation and restoration and most importantly the essential message and power of the gospel of Jesus Christ itself.

Allen quite skillfully corroborates his fundamental discussion of the theology of Cities of refuge and its application to the critical issues of Church discipline, human weakness, grace, redemption, and transformation with an abundance of biblical references from both Old and New Testament.

Rev Dr Hixford Allen's compassionate and pastoral heart shines through in this book. The reader will encounter honesty in self-reflection of his own human condition and Christian pilgrimage and it also demonstrates his interest in those actions and attitudes that need to be adopted in his church to discourage hypocrisy and encourage instead transparent truth telling, open confessing and effective transformation. Dr Allen is not unaware of the risk that this approach engenders but he is confident that the power of grace is greater than the problem of sin. What is noteworthy about this book is that it conveys the conviction that the adoption of this biblical model is not just needed in the church but may be the answer to the untenable situation of recidivism in the wider society where offenders who have paid their debt to society are barred from actively being reintegrated in society because of draconian laws which do not understand the principles inherent in the example of The Cities of Refuge in the Bible. Allen thinks the church should exemplify this and advocate for a more workable approach to this vexing problem in the wider society.

Dr. Samuel Vassell
District Superintendent
Church of the Nazarene
Metro New York District.

BRIEF SUMMARY OF THE TEXT

The church as a safe space for frail people living in an imperfect world is an ongoing concern and debate among church, and nonchurch people. Are humans by nature truly broken and frail? Is this world broken and sinful? Is there a safe space where human frailty or imperfections can be effectively addressed? If so, is the church such a space and what role can the church play in such a process? In this milestone, work *The City of Refuge: God's Gracious Provision for Humanity's Failures and Shortcomings* Dr. Hixford Allen focuses his keen philosophical and theological mind on the gracious practice of the "The City of Refuge," among the Hebrews people as recorded in the Old Testament Scripture. Citing this practice, he argues that it is God's provision for failing individuals to confront, acknowledge and tap into available resources to deal with such failures. This concept he claims reflects God's own nature as is expressed by the experience and words of Psalmist David, "God is our refuge and strength, a very present help in trouble" (Psalm 46:1); "The Lord also will be a refuge for the oppressed, a refuge in times of trouble" (Psalm 9:9).

The similarities in nature of "City of Refuge" and Dr. Allen's understanding of the nature of the church strike him in a way that he suggests that despite the variety of human beliefs and experiences, the believers' life situations, and cultural backgrounds, there is the recurring common factor of human failures. Considering the thoughtful and reflective scholar that he is, Dr. Allen postulates the church as God's contemporary model for human imperfections. He therefore argues that the concept of the City of Refuge which provides grace to those who have failed along the way is taken to its highest level in Christ Jesus, who functions as the head and authority of the church. Jesus is God's ultimate means of grace for fallen humanity – he is the true City of Refuge.

This perspective on the age-old debate of human imperfections, and the broken world will force us to examine our own ecclesiology. Moreso, the role of the church in this broken world. This is an honest quest to offer an answer to what does the church do with those whose imperfections, have overcome their inner drive of wholesomeness that God has created in them? Thanks Dr. Allen, the church "must find ways to reduce and ultimately remove the stigma from those who have repented of wrong doings and demonstrated evidence of transformation."

Dr. Barrington Brown
Senior Pastor
Margate Church of God

CHAPTER 1

THE CASE FOR BUILDING CITIES OF REFUGE

We are imperfect beings living in an imperfect world that is marred by sin and all sorts of maladies. The best of us has situations in our lives that we are not comfortable with and which we struggle to overcome. We have unmet needs, unsolved problems, unresolved issues, weaknesses and shortcomings, disappointments and insecurities, and the list goes on. These imperfections are all around us, and in every one of us. Each person's challenge may be different and may manifest itself in separate ways, but we all have our imperfections and challenges in our lives.

Some imperfections show up in the wrong choices and wrong decisions that people make, the low quality of life that they live, the negative and impure thoughts that they entertain, the unholy feelings that they experience, the immoral behaviors that they practice, and the negative and destructive character traits that are manifested in their lives. For others, imperfections show up in false religious beliefs and practices, pride and arrogance, and lack of love and concern for others.

The responses to our imperfections are diverse. Some individuals accept their imperfections as their lot and make very little effort to deal with them. They leave the future and everything else up to fate – for them, the words of Jay Livingston and Ray Evans' song express their moto in life: "Cay sera, sera, whatever will be will be the future aren't ours to see, cay sera, sera." Others battle with their imperfections and take steps to improve their lives and that of their families. Some individuals, even in the church community, try to get away from the imperfections that are around them. They try to live secluded lives to avoid contact with a world that they feel will contaminate them. They move to what they consider to be a better state or country, with better and safer cities in which to live. Others live in gated Communities, which they hope will keep out unwelcome individuals. They home-school their children to avoid exposing them to the influence of a sinful society. But these individuals soon discover that the contamination they feared is also in the state or country that they immigrated to; and in the cities and communities where they live, as well as in themselves. Some Christians do church shopping, hoping to find a "good church," with good people – a place where they can worship God in spirit and in truth, and grow their children in a good environment. However, while this is a noble effort, there is the common saying, "if you find a perfect church, don't join it; because the moment you do, it is not perfect anymore."

The Laodicean church, (one of the seven churches referred to in the book of revelation) was located in the prosperous city of Laodicea. This city was a banking center. It was known for its garment industry and a medical center noted for ophthalmology. However, the city did not have a good supply of water. Water had to be piped from a hot spring in a distance, and so by the time that the water reached the city of Laodicea it was lukewarm.

The church in the city prided itself on its wealth and delicacies. However, Jesus, the risen Lord, in his message to a church which thought it was doing well said the following:

> You say I am rich, have become wealthy and have need of nothing – and do not know that you are wretched, miserable, poor, blind, and naked. I counsel you to buy from me gold refined in the fire, that you may be rich; and white garments, that you may be clothed, that the shame of your nakedness may not be revealed; and anoint your eyes with eye salve, that you may see (Revelation 3:17, 18).

Like the Laodicean church, we have imperfections and blind spots in our lives that we are not aware of and are not as good as we sometimes think we are.

One of the things that is noticeably clear in the holy scriptures is that all the great leaders (people except Jesus) had flaws and failures: Noah was described as a just and perfect man in his generation and one who walked with God (Genesis 6:9). However, his indiscretion in drinking wine led to drunkenness and nakedness (see Gen 9:20, 21). Abraham is viewed in scripture as the father of faith and is described as a friend of God. However, while he sojourned in Egypt, in his moment of trial he became fearful for his life and he lied about his relationship with his wife, claiming she was his sister (Genesis 12:10-13). The scripture said of Moses: "Now the man Moses was very humble, more than all men who were on the face of the earth" (Numbers 12:3). The Lord also said concerning his relationship with Moses: "If there is a prophet among you, I, the Lord, make myself known to him in a vision; I speak to him in a dream. Not so with my servant Moses, he is faithful in all my house. I speak with him face to face, even plainly, and not in dark sayings; and he sees the form of the Lord" (Numbers 12:6-8). However, Moses murdered an Egyptian in his effort to save his fellow Hebrew, and in anger and frustration at the ingratitude of the children of Israel, he failed to believe and honor the Lord before the people, and it cost him entrance into the promised land of Canaan (see Numbers 20:1-13).

THE CASE FOR BUILDING CITIES OF REFUGE

What have we to say about David, the man after God's own heart, Solomon who the Lord blessed with wisdom, Peter the fearless inner circle disciple of Jesus, Paul, and others of the great servants of the Lord, they all had weaknesses and failures in their lives. Paul, in his letter to the Galatian church, presented and defended the gospel of justification by faith. He argued that a man is placed in a right relationship with God, not by observing the Law, but by faith in the atoning sacrifice of Christ (Galatians 2:16). Justification by faith brings to fore humanity's need for grace, without which he cannot attained a right standing with God. The apostle Paul therefore stated, "I do not set aside the grace of God; for if righteousness comes through the law, then Christ died in vain" (Galatians 2:21). Humankind is flawed and therefore he cannot on his own live to please God.

Much has been done to deal with our imperfections and to make our lives safer and more comfortable. We are inclined to travel in airplanes, motor vehicles and other forms of transportation with an increasing number of safety features. In like manner we have designed and constructed safer roadways, harnessed the use of our technological advancements, precision instruments, computers, and other helpful gadgets, yet we still have accidents; we still make mistakes; and we are far from resolving all our deficiencies. Even with GPS some of us still get lost.

Amidst our advanced learning we still make faulty deductions, draw incorrect inferences, and arrive at wrong conclusions. Many harmful diseases still plague our countries, crime and violence are still rampant in our cities and communities, and the heart of man is still desperately wicked.

We have the perfect, infallible Word of God that provides us with absolute truths. However, our interpretation and application of such truths at times are relative and tentative. It is a fact that in some instances new discoveries which lead to a fuller understanding and application compel us to adjust previously held ideas. Read a few commentaries on some passages of scripture, and there will be such statements as "this is a wrong translation of this word" or "There are two or three views as to what is meant by a particular phrase." Comments like these and others provoke a lot of uncertainties and things that we do not know. The apostle Paul, in contrasting the temporary nature of the gifts of prophecy and tongues with the permanent nature of Love, said it correctly; "For we know in part, and we prophesy in part. . . For now, we see in a mirror dimly; . . .. Now I know in part" (1 Corinthians 13:9, 12).

Jesus' assessment of His disciples' failure to watch with him and stand with him in his moment of need is quite telling of the condition of humanity. Prior to His arrest in the garden of Gethsemane, Jesus said to His disciples, "All of you will be made to stumble because of Me this night, for it is written I will strike the Shepherd, and the sheep of the flock will be scattered" (Matthew 26:31). Peter responded, "Even if all are made to stumble because of You, I will never be made to stumble . . .. Even if I have to die with You, I will not deny You! And so said all the disciples" (Matthew 26:33-35). The scene moved to Gethsemane, and Jesus said to them, "My soul is exceedingly sorrowful, even to death. Stay here and watch with Me" (Matthew 26:38). After moving a little further and praying, Jesus returned to His disciples and found them sleeping. Jesus said to Peter, "What! Could you not watch with me one hour? Watch and pray, lest you enter into temptation. *The spirit indeed is willing, but the flesh is weak"* (Matthew 26:40b, 41). Jesus pointed out that the disciples were willing; they really wanted to watch with their Lord and Master. However, despite their noble intention, and possibly their best effort, they failed to fulfill their pledge, because their flesh was weak.

I recall several years ago; I took my four sons and some other individuals to a church camp several hours from home. I spent all day at the camp site assisting the camp workers to get the campers settled in and to assist with some unforeseen problems that had developed. After a full day's activities, and the night's service, which ended about 10:30pm, I felt quite ok physically, and so a few other individuals who came to assist in setting up the camp, along with myself, decided to travel back home. While I was on my way home, I became extremely tired and sleepy. Unfortunately, I had no other licensed driver with me. We were not near any suitable place to rest – the road being winding, dangerous and dark. Though extremely tired I endeavored to find a safe place to stop and rest. I knew I needed to be awake and alert to navigate the roadway, but my body would not allow me to. I just could not keep myself awake. Despite the danger, I had to stop and get some rest. In the words of Jesus, *my spirit was willing, but my flesh was weak,* when Jesus told the disciples in Gethsemane to watch and pray (Matthew 26:41).

This is the dilemma of humanity. We sometimes know what needs to be done, but do not have the strength or ability to do what is required. We sometimes know where we need to go, but do not know how to get there. Despite our genuine desire to please God and do his bidding, we at times fall short. Despite our best effort and most noble intentions, without God's grace, we at times fail to produce anything that is lasting; let alone solve our most pressing problems or meet our deepest needs.

Living a life without making mistakes or attaining a level of sinless perfection is beyond us in this life. On our own, we just cannot attain such lofty heights. Paul's word in his letter to the Romans is the cry of all humanity without the help of God –

> For I do not understand my own actions, for I do not do what I want, but I do the very thing that I hate. . .. For I have the desire to do what is right, but not the ability to carry it out. For I do not do the good I want, but the evil I do not want is what I keep on doing. . .. Wretched man that I am! Who will deliver me from this body of death? Thanks be to God through Jesus Christ our Lord!" (Romans 7:15-25 ESV).

There are some debates as to the meaning of these words of Paul (Romans 7:14-25). Some believe that Paul is describing (his) pre-conversion experience; others hold that "Paul is writing as a truly regenerate and even mature believer." In addition to these two prominent views, Martyn Lloyd-Jones advocate a third view, he argues that Paul is describing an individual who has experience "conviction but not conversion" and therefore struggles in pursuit of sanctification (John R.W. Stott, 1994, P. 206-207). The focus here is not to try and solve this problem and settle the debate. However, what is not debatable is that we all make mistakes and stumble even after our conversion experience. To be sure, some of us stumble more often than others; some stumble in more areas of their lives than others; and some stumble in the same areas more often than others, but we all stumble at some time or the other. The worst of us need the grace and mercy of God, and the best of us cannot live without it.

While we must make every effort to avoid mistakes and accidents; and while we should hold those who falter accountable; those who fall victim of their own susceptibility to failure and mistakes, and the challenge of living in an imperfect world need some means of grace. They need a place of refuge to run to in their times of need. The bar for Christian living is extremely high, and rightly so; and human expectations are sometimes beyond our ability to meet. Sometimes there is little sympathy for those who fail to live up to expectations. What is expected is a level of perfection of us by others as well as by ourselves without any corresponding means of grace for those who fail in their effort along the way to attain such lofty heights. Such expectations and sentiments are expressed in some of the songs we sing – "Lord; help me to make one hundred; for ninety-nine and one half won't do."

Such a level of sinless perfection (sometimes, expected in our own effort), without the corresponding expression of grace along the way, makes for guilt-ridden lives and marred self-esteem due to the inability to measure up to such lofty standards. This further gives way to lives of pretense and hypocrisy, giving the false impression that the hundred is achieved consistently, when indeed It does not. Others are dying quietly but fail to seek help for fear that no one will understand, and instead of being helped, they will be ridiculed and punished. Consequently, they continue living lives of defeat, guilt, and pain. The standard for Christian living should not be lowered, but there is a need for grace to help in times of need. We all need a "City of Refuge" on our journey of life.

Very early in my early Christian journey, I struggled to control my thought life. Unholy thoughts would come to my mind and even though I did not want to have or entertain them they kept coming. Looking at attractive women in their miniskirts would conjure sensual thoughts in my mind, and it would be a struggle to keep them out. These things never bothered me prior to being a Christian. This continued for a while, and I became so frustrated over the experience that I dread being in the company of such women. I recall crossing the busy street and literally closing my eyes in an effort not to look at such ladies; (I speak the truth; I lie not). This challenge became unbearable, and so I decided to brave up and seek help from my Christian brothers who were more matured in the faith and were further along on the Christian journey. I went to them timidly and fearfully and shared with them my dilemma. To my surprise, the brothers all began to laugh almost unrestrainedly. I was so annoyed and angry. I said to myself; imagine I came to these brothers for help with my challenge and they responded by laughing at me! After about a minute or so, one of the brothers said that they had a similar experience when they started out with the Lord. Then they proceeded to give me sound advice as to how to manage the situation. Immediately the false guilt and burden arising from such temptation were lifted, and with the advice and counsel that were given I overcame it. What brought about the relief more than anything else was not so much the counsel and advice, but the understanding that was communicated in the brothers' response.

They were not judgmental, and they did not condemn me. Their self-disclosure communicated empathy that helped me to resolve my situation. They created for me a 'city of refuge.'

Our world is a global community. Consequently, we influence other cultures, and are influenced by them. Living in a multicultural society like New York, and in other large cities of our world, with people from various cultures can be challenging. The American constitution calls for freedom of speech and justice for all. When this American ideal is coupled with the impact of living in a multicultural society and a global community, where individuals' way of living differs greatly, it becomes extremely difficult (to live up to the demands of political correctness) for the most informed of our society, let alone for others less informed with reference to what is acceptable and what is not acceptable to the various groupings that one has to do with daily. What is perfectly acceptable and normal in one cultural setting may be judged unacceptable in another.

Also, there is the tendency to judge one culture by the laws and ideals of another culture; and to judge 'today's world' by 'yesterday's' laws and ideals, and vice versa. This too is challenging because some things that were acceptable and tolerated say thirty (30) years ago may not be acceptable and tolerated today. Likewise, things that are tolerated and deemed acceptable today may not have been so thirty (30) years ago. Taking this into consideration, one can see how it can be relatively easy to judge a situation wrongly, especially if intent and motivation is not considered.

The challenge is not much easier in the context of religion and of the Christian church with its various denominations. It is exceedingly difficult if not impossible to be true to one's faith and doctrinal beliefs and not offend another group whose belief system is different in some way. What is acceptable to one religion may be offensive in another; and what may be acceptable in one denomination of a particular religion may be unacceptable in another denomination of that same religion. Furthermore, what may be acceptable to one local congregation of a denomination may not be acceptable to another congregation of the same denomination.

In my more than thirty- five (35) years of pastoral ministry, I have the privilege of serving as pastor for four (4) congregations, and serve as supervising pastor for a much larger constituent, all within the same denomination. Over that period, I have received into the fellowship of these churches members from other congregations within the same denomination. It is amazing to see sometimes the significant difference in the way these members understand and practice their faith even though they all share the same doctrinal beliefs and traditions in worship.

In these settings it is relatively easy to offend one another accidentally and unintentionally. Some useful tips that are helpful in avoiding and reducing offence in a multicultural setting includes: cultural awareness and education; respect differences; encourage and practice open communication; avoid stereotyping; be aware of nonverbal cues; be cautious with humor; learn conflict resolution skills; and stay informed with current events and cultural issues. Studying and practicing the "one another" passages in the bible is of paramount importance if we are to reduce offending one another. It is no secret, however, that most people living together are not aware of these and other useful tips, and those who are aware of them do not always practice them. All these argue for tolerance, understanding and a spirit of forgiveness – some means of grace are needed for individuals who share common space and facilities, to live together in harmony with one another.

The American society is a very litigious one. Frivolous lawsuits are the order of the day. Lawyers and their clients search for the minutest infractions to face the jury and the judge. In such instances no regard or understanding is given to genuine mistakes or the unintentionality of actions. Mercy is thrown through the door, and every opportunity is sought to claim the proverbial 'Pound of flesh.'

An individual's life can be totally ruined over a slight and genuine mistake or accident with little opportunity to recover.

Despite man's imperfections, he expects perfection from others and at times from himself. Such unrealistic expectations show up in marriages – couples expect perfection from their spouses, and sometimes end up divorce for simple things. Citizens expect perfection from their governmental leaders; society expects perfection from parents in the parenting of their children. Many children are taken from the homes of their parents and guardians over simple indiscretions and genuine mistakes and are placed in foster care that in some cases is a far worse situation. Perfection is expected of Christians in general, and Christian leaders in particular. Make no mistake, individuals should be held accountable for their actions, and in particular, leaders must be held accountable by the people they serve, and by those who place them in their respective offices. A moto of mine is that every position of honor demands responsible behavior. However, the concern here is not with accountability, but rather with the lack of understanding and compassion, and at times mindless and heartless response to genuine mistakes and unintentional actions that cause hurt and pain. As fallen creatures, we need cities of refuge to help us on our journey of life; we need cities of refuge to survive.

CHAPTER 2

THE CITY OF REFUGE IN SCRIPTURE

The children of Israel were living in slavery in Egypt for over four hundred years. During that period, their lives were governed by the rules and laws of their task masters. Justice was taken from them, and they were at the mercy of their merciless oppressors. They had to endure the unfair treatment that was mitered out to them. They were placed under forced labor that was difficult and burdensome. Their sons were taken from the bosoms of their mothers and care givers and slaughtered before their eyes; and their dignity as a people was shattered.

Several hundred years prior, the Lord had made a promise to Abraham: "Then He said to Abram: know certainly that your descendants will be strangers in a land that is not theirs, and will serve them, and they will afflict them four hundred years. And also, the nation whom they serve I will judge; afterward, they shall come out with great possessions" (Genesis 15:13, 14). At the appointed time, the Lord remembered his promise to Abraham, Isaac, and Jacob. He called Moses and commissioned him to be his instrument of deliverance, to bring the children of Israel out of Egypt's bondage. "And the Lord said: I have surely seen the oppression of my people who are in Egypt, and have heard their cry because of their taskmasters, for I know their sorrow. So, I have come down to deliver them out of the hand of the Egyptians, and to bring them up from that land to a good and large land . . .. Come now, therefore, and I will send you to Pharaoh that you may bring, My people, the children of Israel, out of Egypt" (Exodus 3:7-10). The Lord judged Egypt, and by the hand of Moses delivered the children of Israel out of Egypt's bondage.

Our God is a deliverer. He still sees the sufferings of his people, the unjust treatment that is metered out to them. He still hears their cry for help, and He still comes down and delivers them.

The Lord is also a God of justice – "the eyes of the Lord are in every place, keeping watch on the evil and the good" (Proverbs 15:3). Whenever and wherever he sees injustice, He takes steps to correct it. As he did for the children of Israel, so he will do for all his children.

Moses, by the leading of the Lord (in a pillar of cloud by day and a pillar of fire by night) brought the children of Israel out of Egypt; led them through the Red Sea; fed them with manna; gave them water from the rock; and led them through the wilderness to Mount Sinai to meet with God. The Lord had told Moses, "When you have brought the people out of Egypt, you shall serve God on this mountain" (Exodus 3:12).

At Mount Sinai the Lord made a covenant with Israel. "And Moses went up to God, and the Lord called to him from the mountain, saying, thus you shall say to the house of Jacob, and tell the children of Israel: you have seen what I did to the Egyptians, and how I bore you on eagle's wings and brought you to myself. Now therefore, if you will indeed obey my voice and keep my covenant, then you shall be a special treasure to me above all people; for all the earth is mine. And you shall be to me a kingdom of priests and a holy nation" (Exodus 19:3-6).

The Lord was about to make the children of Israel into a 'kingdom of priests and holy nation.' From there on, they were to be governed not by the laws of Egypt from where the Lord had delivered them, nor by the laws of the land that they were going to possess. They were to be governed by the laws of the Lord who delivered them; godly laws which reflect love for God and love for their fellowmen. By the hand of Moses, the Lord gave his people His laws by which they should live (details of which are in Exodus chapter 20:1- 24:8). These laws include the Ten Commandments and the laws contained in the Book of the Covenant.

The Decalogue or Ten Commandments take the form or style of "apodictic laws consisting of positive and negative commands ("you shall . . ., you shall not); while the 'Book of the Covenant' contains mainly casuistic laws (and some apodictic laws). The casuistic or case laws are set forth in the "if" and "then" clauses – ('if a man . . ., then . . .'). These casuistic laws imply among other things that infraction is possible and likely even among God's covenant people – accident can and do happen among the people of God. They give directions as to what should be done when there is any infraction. These laws together with the Decalogue provide the guiding principles for life in community (as God's covenant people) and ensure the purity of the worship of Jehovah and that justice is done under the old covenant. Like Israel, the people of God having been delivered from sin's bondage, the tyranny of sin and are called to live differently – "Therefore, if anyone is in Christ, he is a new creation; old things have passed away; behold, all things have become new" (2 Corinthians 5:17). The New walk with God calls for a new way of living; that is guided by different principles, set by our new Lord and master. While we should obey the laws of the countries in which we live, the law of God takes priority whenever there is any conflict.

Luke recorded the account of the healing of a lamed man by Peter and John. This was followed by the preaching of the gospel in the name of Jesus. However, the religious leaders were disturbed by them preaching in the name of Jesus, whom Peter said, "you crucified," and so they charged Peter and John "not to speak at all nor teach in the name of Jesus. But Peter and John answered and said to them, whether it is right in the sight of God to listen to you more than to God, you judge" (Acts 4: 18, 19).

Exodus 21:1, 12-14:

The first biblical reference to the idea of a city of refuge is found among the collection of laws in Exodus 20:22 through 23:33 referred to as "The Book of the Covenant" (Exodus 24:7). The Lord instructed Moses concerning the rules that he should give to Israel, his chosen people who would represent him to the world.

> Now these are the rules that you shall set before then . . .. Whoever strikes a man so that he dies shall be put to death. But if he did not lie in wait for him, but God let him fall into his hand, then I will appoint for you a place to which he may flee. But if a man acts with premeditation against his neighbor, to kill him by treachery, you shall take him from my altar, that he may die (Exodus 21:1, 12, 13).

According to this text, the Lord promised that he would appoint a place of safety for a person who kills someone unintentionally to run to for refuge. However, such place of safety should not accommodate those guilty of premediated killing. A clear distinction is made between intentional and unintentional killing, and the way justice should be conducted in each case.

The place appointed by the Lord to which the slayer should run was not named. Greenberg considers such a place different from the altar. He stated that, "the nature of this place is not further defined, it being clear only that it is other than the altar of YHWH which is referred to in vs. 14. For that verse says that the murderer is to be taken away for execution even from the altar; evidently, then, the aforementioned place is not that altar" (Greenberg, p. 125). However, it is not clear from the cited text that the place appointed by God was different from the altar. It could also be inferred from the Exodus 21:12-14 that the altar was that place appointed by God, but such place should not accommodate murderers. Murphy supported this point. In his comment on the text, he said,

> The murderer, as he acts from malice . . . is here, by way of contrast with the milder sentence of the premeditating manslayer, emphatically condemned to death, from which not even the altar of God, much less the city of refuge, shall shelter him. This indicates both the fact that the altar was already regarded as a sacred and almost inviolable asylum for the defenseless, on account of its intimate connection with the Supreme Being" (Murphy, 1868, p. 251-252).

Greenberg further stated, however, that "The law of Exodus, speaking of an altar, is compared with the flight of Adonijah and Joab into the tent sanctuary of Jerusalem, (I Kings 1:50, 2:28). With good reason it is supposed that the law of Exodus reflects the earliest custom of seeking asylum at the local sanctuaries that filled ancient Palestine before the Josianic reform. The vague 'place' of the Exodus Law is accordingly interpreted to mean sanctuary site" (Greenberg, p. 126). Although it is not clear from this text as to the place that the Lord appointed for the slayer to run to for safety, what is clear is that the Lord did appoint a place of refuge. The Lord did make special provision for the safety of those who kill unintentionally.

The slayer had to run to the place appointed by God to escape from the avenger of blood. Israel's justice system at the time, require that the *'go'el'* assumes the responsibility to avenge the death of his family member. The Hebrew word *'go'el* (avenger) "Was used of someone acting in the interest of the family to free another from slavery, to purchase land to keep it within the family, even to perform

THE CITY OF REFUGE

the duty of a Levirate, as well as of someone who pursues and executes the killer of a family member" (The New Interpreter's Dictionary of the Bible, Vol.1, 2006, p. 357). In so doing, the *go'el* would restore honor and dignity to the family of the deceased. Without city of refuge the avenger of blood may pursue and kill an innocent person who was not guilty of death because his action which caused the death was unintentional and not premeditated.

The point is also made that in addition to the act being unintentional, it was the doing of God's providential work. This text accorded the unintentional slaying of the man to the providential work of God – "but God let him fall into his hand." The implication of the phrase "but God let him fall into his hand" may be that the slayer is himself, the Lord's instrument of judgment on the slain, or the slaying was an 'act of God,' the consequence of living in a fallen and imperfect world. Paul stated that civil authorities are appointed by God and acts with his authority in rewarding the good and punishing evil:

> Do you want to be afraid of the authority? Do what is good, and you will have praise from the same. For he is God's minister to you for good. But if you do evil, be afraid; for he does not bear the sword in vain; for he is God's minister, an avenger to execute wrath on him who practices evil (Romans 13:3b, 4).

In either case, the Lord appoints a place of refuge for the slayer – such act of slaying should be treated differently from intentional killing, which is murder.

There are several passages which accord what seems to be an accident to God's doing. One of such passages is that which surrounds Sampson wanting to take a philistine wife. Samson saw a Philistine woman and asked his parents to get the woman for him to be his wife. Although this action seemed to be out of line for a leader of the people of Israel it seemed that the Lord was using such an action to accomplish his purpose. The recorded account reads:

> Now Samson went down to Timnah and saw a woman in Timnah of the daughter of the Philistines. So, he went up and told his father and mother, saying, I have seen a woman in Timnah, of the daughters of the Philistines; now therefore, get her for me as a wife. Then his father and mother said to him, is there no woman among the daughters of your brethren, or among all my people that you must go and get a wife from the uncircumcised Philistines? And Samson said to his father, get her for me for she pleases me well. But his father and mother did not know that it was of the Lord - that he was seeking an occasion to move against the Philistines. For at that time the Philistines had dominion over Israel (Judges 14:1-4).

This passage revealed that Samson action of taking a wife from among the daughters of his enemies was going to serve a divine purpose. Samson himself was not aware that "it was of the Lord," neither were his parents. He did not sit down and planned that he was going to use the occasion to instigate a fight with the Philistines. One could say that the whole thing was an accident: or that through this action God let the philistines fall into his hand. God used the occasion and what followed as an opportunity to use Samson as his instrument of Judgment on the Philistines. If you please, the Lord let the Philistines fall into the hand of Samson.

This passage in Exodus revealed that the Lord made a distinction between intentional killing and unintentional killing. He appointed a place of refuge for those who kill someone unintentionally to flee for safety. However, such a place of safety should not be made available for murders. The implication of this text is that unintentional injury is possible even among the people of God, and when such occur, it should be treated differently from an act that caused injury that was premeditated. The passage also implied that the Lord is a God of justice. While those who kill unintentionally should not suffer death, those who kill intentionally should not be given refuge in the place that the Lord had appointed. The innocent should not be punished nor should the guilty be set free.

Numbers 35:6, 9-34

The next biblical passage that provides information on the city of refuge is found in the book of Numbers. The children of Israel received the revelation of God's law, and under God's direction they erected the tabernacle. The cloud that guided them lifted from above the tabernacle and the children of Israel set out on their journey, the Lord leading them by a pillar of cloud by day and a pillar of fire by night. Their journey was marked by grumbling and complaining against God, and against Moses and Aaron. Instead of putting their trust in the Lord who delivered them from bondage, they kept looking back whenever they faced a challenge. Manny died in the wilderness because of their rebellion and disobedience, and lack of faith in God and in His appointed leaders.

However, Moses led them and brought them to the plain of Moab. Moses then, under the direction of the Lord, began to prepare them (the new generation) to enter the land of Canaan. As a part of their preparation, Moses again, under the direction of the Lord gave then instructions regarding the city of refuge. Additional information concerning cities of refuge is given in the book of Numbers. This passage reads:

> And the Lord spoke to Moses in the plains of Moab by the Jordan across from Jericho, saying. . .. The cities that you give to the Levites shall be six cities of refuge, where you shall permit the manslayer to

flee.... And the Lord spoke to Moses, saying, speak to the people of Israel and say to them, when you cross the Jordan into the Land of Canaan, then you shall select cities of refuge for you that the manslayer who kills any person without intent may flee there. The cities shall be for you a refuge from the avenger that the man slayer may not die until he stands before the congregation for judgment. And the cities that you give shall be six cities of refuge. You shall give three cities beyond the Jordan and three cities in the land of Canaan, to be cities of refuge. These six cities shall be for refuge for the people of Israel, and for the stranger and for the sojourner among them, that anyone who kills any person without intent may flee there. . ... But if he pushed him suddenly without enmity or hurled anything on him without lying in wait or use a stone that could cause death, and without seeing him dropped it on him, so that he dies, though he was not his enemy and did not seek his harm, then the congregation shall judge between the manslayer and the avenger of blood, in accordance with these rules. And the congregation shall rescue the manslayer from the hand of the avenger of blood, and the congregation shall restore him to his city of refuge to which he had fled, and he shall live in it until the death of the high priest who was anointed with the holy oil. But if the manslayer shall at any time go beyond the boundaries of his city of refuge, and the avenger of blood kills the manslayer, he shall not be guilty of blood. For he must remain in his city of refuge until the death of the high priest, but after the death of the high priest the manslayer may return to the land of his possession. And these things shall be for a statue and rule for you throughout your generations in all your dwelling places. . . .. And you shall accept no ransom for him who has fled to his city of refuge that he may return to dwell in the land before the death of the high priest. You shall not pollute the land in which you live, for blood pollutes the land, and no atonement can be made for the land for the blood that is shed in it, except by the blood of the one who shed it. You shall not defile the land in which you live, in the midst of which I dwell, for I the Lord dwell in the midst of the people of Israel (Numbers 35:6, 9-34).

This passage is the first place in scripture that the term 'City of Refuge' appeared, although the concept was already present in the passage in Exodus 21:13. The following additional information concerning the cities of refuge can be drawn from this passage:

- The cities of refuge were cities given to the Levites or manned by the Levites (35:6)
- The number of the cities of refuge and their locations – six cities of refuge, three beyond the Jordan and three in the land of Canaan they were all over the land of Israel (35:6, 13, 14)
- The command given to select cities of refuge when they enter the land of Canaan (35:9-11)
- That the cities of refuge shall be a place of refuge for the manslayer from the avenger to ensure that he stand trial before the congregation (35:12)
- That the congregation has the responsibility to see to the safety of the slayer who kills another unintentionally.
- Examples of what constitutes unintentional killing.
- The individuals who should be accommodated in the cities of refuge – the cities of refuge should be a place of refuge for "the people of Israel, and the stranger and for the sojourner

among them" – all who meet the stated law should have access to the city of refuge (35:15)
- That the cities of refuge shall not accommodate murderers, but only those who kill unintentionally and accidentally (35:16-24)
- That after the death of the high priest the slayer may return to the land of his possession (35:28)
- That no ransom shall be accepted for the manslayer that fled to a city of refuge to permit him to return to the land of his possession before the death of the high priest (35:32).

Cities of refuge are about justice and grace mingled together. It is noteworthy that the manslayer should stand trial, he was not allowed to remain in the city of refuge without a trial and he is being found innocent of intentional killing – justice must be sought and carried out. Those who are guilty of intentional killing should be punished and those who kill unintentionally should be shown mercy. There should be more than one witness to convict a supposed murderer – "the murderer shall be put to death on the testimony of witnesses; but one witness is not sufficient testimony against a person for the death penalty" (Numbers 35:30). Every effort should be made to make sure that justice is done. Without cities of refuge the innocent manslayer may be killed by the avenger of blood without the opportunity of a fair trial, and without a fair trial the guilty may be set free.

Very importantly also, is the fact that although the slayer's action was unintentional, he could not return to his normal life in his possession forthwith; he had to remain in the city of refuge until the death of the high priest who was serving at the time. The man slayer was not guilty of death because his action was not intentional. However, the death that he caused must be atoned for. To allow the manslayer to return to his possession without atonement for the slain would be tantamount to defiling the land (35:33). Until the death of the high priest, his only place of safety is in the city of refuge. "This concept indicates that the high priest represented all who sought refuge and bore the iniquity of the spilled blood to his own grave. By doing this he released the manslayer from the burden of accountability" (Six Cities of refuge, http://bridgetothebible.com/Bible%20Lists/6%20cities%20of%20refuge.htm, p. 5of 7).

This point of the manslayer remaining in the city of refuge until the death of the high priest also places emphasis on the sacredness of life. Even though the death was caused by an unintentional action, the person who caused such death must bear some responsibility. The action that caused the death may be accidental and unintentional, but it resulted in the death of an individual, and caused severe grief, pain, and loss to the deceased loved ones. It may also have been the result of the slayers own carelessness and susceptibility to failure. Consequently, he cannot be allowed to get back to normal living as though what has happened should be taken lightly.

The Lord God had said previously to Noah that, "Surely for your lifeblood I will demand a reckoning, from the hand of every beast, I will require it, and from the hand of man. From the hand of every man's brother, I will require the life of man. Whoever sheds man's blood. By man, his blood shall be shed; for in the image of God he made man" (Genesis 9:5,6). Therefore, since the atonement for the slain was not made with the slayer's blood, the protection given to him in the city of refuge was an act of grace. The man slayer was not kept in the city of refuge mainly because he was not to bear any blame for the death he caused, but mainly because of grace and compassion extended to him who was unable based on his imperfection and susceptibility to failure to avoid such tragedy.

Among the common sayings that are uttered when someone causes hurt to another is: 'it is not your fault,' or society is to be blamed. Several individuals have been killed by other people who thought that their lives were in danger, when the facts of the case later revealed that there was no real danger. Example – someone was killed by another who wrongly thought that the victim had a gun or some other weapon. Or it could be that a child had a terrible upbringing which resulted in severe emotional and mental scars, and as a result commit murders which some may see as the result of his or her painful upbringing.

However, even though one should acknowledge the shortcomings of an individual, and the impact of others or society on such individual's action, the one that cause harm and death to another is not without blame and should bear some responsibility for his/her action. The story was told of a man who was a drunkard and who had two sons. His two sons grew up, one became a drunkard like his father, and the other did not. Both sons were asked what led them to make the decision regarding drinking excessively. The one who became a drunkard said, he became a drunkard because his father was a drunkard. The other son who did not drink excessively said he did not drink excessively because his father was a drunkard. We all have the power of choice and are most responsible for our actions. To free the person who causes hurt from all responsibility would be to dehumanize such a one. Such an action would imply that the person who caused harm to another was acting as a robot without the power to choose and decide on his actions.

The word of God in the book of Ezekiel relative to the watchman's action and God's judgment of those who sinned is relevant to this point. The Lord said to the prophet Ezekiel that if He make someone a watchman and commissioned him to watch; "if the watchman fails to warn the people, the people will die for their sins, but the Lord will require the blood of the people from the watchman's hand" (Ezekiel 33:6). Note well what the scripture said, "the people will die for their sin" – they are responsible for their action even though the watchman failed to warn them. Consequently, as is the case of the manslayer in the city of refuge. His being accommodated in the city of refuge is not indicative of him not bearing any responsibility for the death he caused. His being accommodated is an act of grace. Our safety in the city of refuge is an act of grace. When as individuals we experience the protection of God, it is more about the grace and goodness of God than that we are fully deserving of such acts of kindness.

The time that the slayer spend in the city of refuge is related to the time of the death of the reigning high priest at the time. It is therefore, controlled providentially by the Lord, since the Lord is the one who sets the boundaries for our lives. Some slayers will spend a relatively short time in confinement if the reigning high priest dies shortly after he ran for safety in the city of refuge. Others will spend a long time in the city of refuge if the reigning high priest lives for a long time thereafter. God providentially determine when the slayer is properly prepared and ready to reenter the general society. This has implication for atonement and rehabilitation. One is only sufficiently prepared for life in the community and fellowship with his Maker when one's sin has been atoned for and such atonement has been appropriated. Time spent in the city of refuge also speaks to a time of rehabilitation. The slayer is prepared spiritually, mentally, emotionally, and otherwise, to facilitate a smooth reentry into the community. The Matter of justification and sanctification are also implied. In justification one is acquitted of the charges, declared righteous based on the shed blood of Jesus, and placed in a right standing with God. Through sanctification the justified one seeks to make practical in his daily life what he is positionally in God.

The cities of refuge were to be in the land where the people of God lived. This is significant for two reasons: firstly, unintentional killing/accidents can and will happen (even) among the people of God. Being a part of the family of God, does not make believers immune to accidents and failures. For sure, we have the help of the Holy Spirit, but our weak use of God's strength makes accidents possible among members of the faith community. ("And if the righteous is scarcely saved, what will become of the ungodly and the sinner" (1 Peter 4:18). We hurt people unintentionally, sometimes without even knowing it. We sometimes unintentionally offend and hurt others with our words and actions. We sometimes do so because of our susceptibility to failure and mistakes; and, because of our immaturity and imperfections. James in his epistle discussed the challenge of teachers owing to the difficulty of controlling our speech. James said, "for we all stumble in many things. If anyone does not stumble in word, he is a perfect man, able to bridle the whole body" (James 3:2). With all our good and most noble intentions and our best efforts, accidents do happen.

The cities of refuge were located at strategic locations in the promised land of Canaan. This is to ensure accessibility; wherever the tragedy of unintentional killing happen, there should be a city of refuge close enough to enable the manslayer to flee to. These cities of refuge should also be made available to "the stranger, and for the sojourner among them" (35:15). There should be no discrimination against non-Jews. God is the God and Judge of the whole earth, and not just for the children of Israel. Whoever runs to the city of refuge, being innocent of intentional killing should be accommodated.

Deuteronomy 4:41-43; 19:1-13:

The next biblical reference that provides information on the city of refuge occurred in the book of Deuteronomy (4:41-43; 19:1-13). The setting is somewhat like that of the passage in numbers. The new generation is in the final year of wondering. The old generation (all those who were twenty years and older when they left Egypt) save Joshua and Caleb have died during the journey/wondering in the wilderness. The laws that God gave to the children of Israel at Mount Sinai are repeated to the new generation. For one final time before they enter the land of Canaan, Moses again reminded

THE CITY OF REFUGE

the new generation of God's law regarding the city of refuge. The passage reads:

> When the Lord your God has cut off the nations whose land the Lord your God is giving you, and you dispossess them and dwell in their cities and in their houses, you shall separate three cities for yourself in the midst of your land which the Lord your God is giving you to possess. You shall prepare roads for yourself and divide into three parts the territory of your land which the Lord your God is giving you to inherit, that any manslayer may flee there. And this is the case of the manslayer who flees there, that he may live: whoever kills his neighbor unintentionally, not having hated him in the past – as when a man goes to the woods with his neighbor to cut timber, and his hand swings a stroke with the ax to cut down the tree, and the head slips from the handle and strikes his neighbor so that he dies – he shall flee to one of these cities and live; lest the avenger of blood, while his anger is hot, pursue the manslayer and overtake him, because the way is long, and kill him, though he was not deserving of death since he has not hated the victim in the past.
>
> Therefore, I command you, saying, you shall separate three cities for yourself. Now if the Lord your God enlarges your territory, as he swore to your fathers, and gives you the Land which he promised to give to your fathers, and if you keep all these commandments and do them, which I command you today, to love the Lord your God and to walk always in his ways, then you shall add three more cities for yourselves besides these three, lest innocent blood be

shed in the midst of your land which the Lord your God is giving you as an inheritance, and thus guilt of bloodshed be upon you. But if anyone hates his neighbor, lies in wait for him, rises against him and strikes him mortally, so that he dies, and he flees to one of these cities, then the elders of his city shall send and bring him from there and deliver him over to the hand of the avenger of blood, that he may die. Your eyes shall not pity him, but you shall put away the guilt of innocent blood from Israel, that it may go well with you (Deuteronomy 19:1-13).

Roads were to be prepared for the manslayer to flee to the city of refuge. The roads leading to the city of refuge should not be long (implied in 19:6b); and the names of the cities of refuge are mentioned (4:41-43). Boice posited that "nonbiblical sources tell us that the aid to these fugitives was even more extensive. Bridges were built over ravines, so the fugitive could take the shortest route possible. The roads were carefully repaired each spring. At every crossroads, special signs read, Refuge! Refuge! No one wanted a fugitive to take the wrong road. Moreover, the signs were made large, so that even a man who was running hard could read them without stopping" (Boyce, 2006, p. 111). All these efforts imply that easy access to the city of refuge should be provided, to ensure that the manslayer would reach the city of refuge and not be overtaken by the avenger of blood.

This passage reiterated the point previously made in the Exodus 21:12-14 – that those who kill unintentionally and accidentally were not deserving of death and should run to the city of refuge for safety. But those who willfully kill another should not be accommodated in the city of refuge. They should not be pitied; instead, such persons should be handed over to the avenger of blood to be punished for their crime.

The person who kills another unintentionally is not deserving of death (19:6). Failure to see to the building of cities of refuge, resulting in the shedding of innocent blood, that is, the killing of the slayer who accidentally and unintentionally kills another, will incur the guilt of innocent blood on the community. Likewise, seeing the just punishment of a murderer will free the community of the guilt of the blood of the innocent person that was murdered (19:11-13). Allowing the punishment of the innocent and or the setting free of the guilty will both incur guilt of innocent blood on the community. Justice must be carried out.

This passage reinforces the point that protection must be provided to those who accidentally and unintentionally kill someone, and punishment must be metered out to the guilty. This was a divine command that the people of God should make every effort to obey. The wellbeing of the community depends on obeying this command to the building of cities of refuge and on the proper use of such cities – "that it may go well with you" (19:13b).

Joshua 20:1-9:

The last Old Testament text that deals extensively with the command to build cities of refuge is found in the book of Joshua chapters 20:1-9. The children of Israel are now in the land of promise. Most of the land to the west of the Jordan have been conquered and allotted to the various tribes. God's chosen people could now experience relative rest from their enemies, and settle down, each under his own fig tree and enjoy the blessings of being in the Promised Land of Canaan. The Lord spoke to Joshua, their leader, and once more addressed the issue of the building of cities of refuge.

> The Lord also spoke to Joshua, saying, speak to the children of Israel, saying: appoint for yourselves cities of refuge, of which I spoke to you through Moses,

that the slayer who kills a person accidentally or unintentionally may flee there; and they shall be your refuge from the avenger of blood.

And when he flees to one of those cities and stands at the entrance of the gate of the city and declares his case in the hearing of the elders of that city, they shall take him into the city as one of them and give him a place that he may dwell among them. Then if the avenger of blood pursues him, they shall not deliver the slayer into his hand, because he struck his neighbor unintentionally but did not hate him beforehand. And he shall dwell in that city until he stands before the congregation for judgment, and until the death of the one who is high priest in those days. Then the slayer may return and come to his own city and his own house, to the city from which he fled. So, they appointed Kedesh in Galilee, in the mountains of Naphtali, Shechem in the mountains of Ephraim, and Kirjath Arba (which is Hebron) in the mountains of Judah. And on the other side of the Jordan, by Jericho eastward, they assigned Bezer in the wilderness on the plain, from the tribe of Ruben, Ramoth in Gilead, from the tribe of Gad, and Golan in Bashan, from the tribe of Manasseh. These were the cities appointed for the children of Israel and for the stranger who dwelt among them, that whoever kills a person accidentally might flee there, and not die at the hand of the avenger of blood until he stood before the congregation (Joshua 20:1-9).

THE CITY OF REFUGE

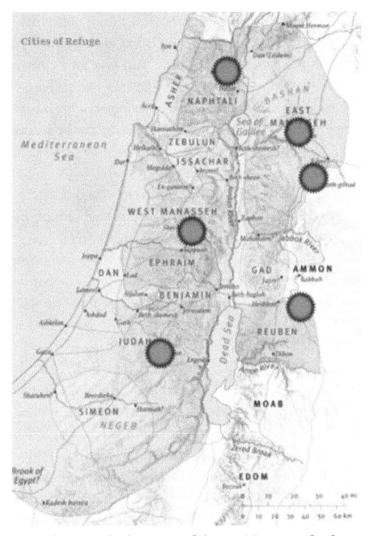

Map showing the location of the six (6) cities of refuge.

This passage served as a final reminder to the children of Israel to build cities of refuge, and therefore underscored the importance of cities of refuge. In this passage, the Lord instructed Joshua to carry out the instructions that he gave Moses concerning the building of cities of refuge. This passage for the most part reiterated previously given information regarding the city of refuge, along with the names and location of all six cities of refuge. It is also stated in this passage that when the innocent manslayer runs to the city of refuge, "and declares his case in the hearing of the elders of that city, they shall take him into the city as one of them, and give him a place, that he may dwell among them" (20:4). The implication here is that the innocent slayer should be treated as a bona fide member of the community within the city of refuge. He must not be treated as a prisoner or as some second-class citizen of the city. He should be given a place to live and be treated well.

These four biblical passages underscore and highlight the importance of building cities of refuge in the land of promise. The command to build cities of refuge was repeated four (4) times. They were commanded to build cities of refuge at the establishment of the covenant at Mount Sanai. Central to be God's covenant people and living in community with one another is the building of cities of refuge. They were reminded after their forty (40) years of wondering in the wilderness (and just about all the old generation that left Egypt (except Moses, Joshua, and Caleb) had died. Those present at the time were either children when the command to build cities of refuge was first given, or they were yet unborn. They were again reminded in the plain of Moab during their final preparation to enter the Promised Land. Moses took the time in his final word before he died to remind the new generation of the commandments of the Lord and challenged them to obey the Lord that it may be go well with them. Now they are in the Promised Land, and the Lord again through Joshua, reminded the children of Israel one final time to build cities of refuge.

The people of God must not forget the importance of having cities of refuge among them; to do so would be to run the risk of polluting the land with the shedding of innocent blood. The leaders should see to it that this is done; their task as leaders is not complete without it. No faith community is complete without a 'city of refuge.' Provision must be made to protect the cause of the innocent by providing means of grace that those who cause pain and suffering due to their weaknesses and susceptibility to failure may continue to live.

From the leading Old Testament texts on the city of refuge (exodus 21:13; Numbers 35:6, 9-34; Deuteronomy 19:1-13; and Joshua 20:1-9) we can draw the following conclusions:

- Cities of refuge were appointed by God for the safety of those who accidentally and unintentionally cause death to others.
- Cities of refuge are not for the protection of murderers and should not accommodate them.
- Cities of refuge were ordered to ensure that justice takes place in the land – that the innocent be not condemned with the guilty, and the guilty be not set free.
- Cities of refuge were means of grace extended to individuals to meet their shortcomings due to their imperfections, and their living in an imperfect world.
- Cities of refuge are necessary in the community of God's people.
- Cities of refuge is an acknowledgment that accidents will happen even among the people of God, and when they do happen, they should be treated differently from harm resulting from intentional actions.

The city of refuge should ensure that justice is done, it is a safeguard against the injustice, and that there is not excessive punishment for actions that caused pain, hurt and death, but was not deliberate or intentional. These passages bring to the fore the importance of motive in deciding the course of action (in this case punishment) that should be applied when someone causes hurt or pain to another individual. While actions are certainly important and should be taken seriously, of great or even greater importance is the motive or attitude that gave rise to such actions.

Jesus addressed this matter of motive in the Sermon on the Mount when he dealt with the "you have heard it said" clauses. Those guilty of adultery were not only the ones that who committed the act, but also those "who look at a woman to lust for her" (Matthew 5:28). Jesus also associated the matter of purer motive with the "righteousness that exceeds that of the Pharisee. Those who give their charitable deeds and offer prayers with the intent of attracting the praise of men are viewed as hypocrites, and such have no reward of their heavenly father (see Matthew 61ff.). The crowning purpose and central message of the city of refuge and that to which it points is grace – it is our gracious God extending grace to his creatures – "He has not dealt with us according to our sins, nor punish us according to our iniquities. For as the heavens are high above the earth, so great is His mercy toward those who fear Him. . .. **For He knows our frame; He remembers that we are dust**: (Psalm 103:10-14). The Lord knows that we will make mistakes. He does not want us to sin, but he knows that because of our frailty it is likely that we will, and so he makes provision for our shortcomings. We are invited to come boldly to the throne of grace that we might find grace to help in our times of need (Hebrews 4:16). The city of refuge was not put in place for perfect people – innocent, but not perfect. It was not put in place to protect the "perfect ones" from those who seek to do them harm. Rather it was put in place for the protection of those who fail because of their imperfections.

CHAPTER 3

THE CITY OF REFUGE – GOD'S PROVISION FOR HUMAN WEAKNESS

The word of God sets forth God as our refuge: "God is our refuge and strength, a very present help in trouble" (Psalm 46:1); "The Lord also will be a refuge for the oppressed, a refuge in times of trouble" (Psalm 9:9). The idea communicated from the use of the word 'refuge' in these psalms is that of a place of security from danger; or a place of high fortifications to which those in danger may escape to. Both verses (Psalm 9:9; and 46:1) remind us that God is our refuge and strength. We can rely on him to be our protector and defender, and we can trust in him to keep us safe from harm. Whether we are facing challenging times or just need someone to turn to for comfort and support.

The Lord is a refuge for the poor and needy, the slaves and bonded laborers; the orphans and widows, and so he made provisions for them to live among his people. The laws regarding the year of jubilee also communicate the idea that the Lord is a refuge to the oppressed. At that time, slaves should be set free, their lands returned to them, and their debts cancelled. The deist presents God as the creator of the universe and its natural laws but is not intricately involve in the affairs of life. However, the psalmist presents our God as a present help. When his people are in trouble, they can call upon him, and run to him for refuge. Those who do will experience his protection and care – because "He who dwells in the secret place of the Most High shall abide under the shadow of the Almighty" (Psalm 91:1).

The cities of refuge were a divine response/accommodation for human weaknesses. God knew that we would face various challenges in our lives which are beyond our natural ability to overcome, even with our best effort. Consequently, he made provision for us. Provision is made for our sins to be forgiven (I John 1:9; 2:1, 2); provision is made for us to fulfill the mission that he has committed to our trust (Luke 24:49; Acts 1:6-8); and provision is made for us to continue to live despite our faults and failures. You do not have to be perfect to live. The Lord commanded that those who unintentionally fail may run to the city of refuge and find help in their times of need.

The dilemma of humanity is that he is imperfect, and he lives in an imperfect world. However, the world in which he lives is increasingly demanding perfection from him, and despite his best effort he is unable to meet such demand. Some individuals, because of the constant pressure to be perfect, have come to require such perfection from themselves. They not only require perfection from themselves but end up condemning themselves and others for not being perfect.

As a Pentecostal believer, who believe in the baptism of the Holy Spirit as a subsequent experience to conversion; after conversion I was encouraged to pray and fast earnestly for the Pentecostal experience. As young converts we were told that if any sin were in our lives such sin would hinder us from having the experience – (you need to be perfect to receive the baptism of the Holy Spirit). What is more, we were told by some older believers that the same thing that prevents us from receiving the experience will prevent us from entering heaven. This moved the baptism of the Holy Spirit out of the realm of being a gift from God to something to be earned. Let me hasten to say that

I do not believe that those who practice a life of sin will receive the experience. The experience is for those who repent of their sins and turn away from it to God (Acts 2:38-39).

I did everything possible to gain this experience. If a sinful thought crossed my mind during the day; or if I slip up in any way, I will not expect to receive the experience. For me then, I had to be perfect to receive the gift of God. I struggled for over a year and six months trying to be perfect until a deacon at the church counseled with me and told me that I will not be good enough for the gift of God, I must receive the gift of God by putting faith in God and his word. It was then that my breakthrough came.

Again, let me say that living in sin and in rebellion against God will hinder a believer from having the experience of the baptism of the Holy Spirit or any such blessing that God's word promises. The divine and the human element must be held in tension. The baptism of the Holy Spirit is a gift from God, a privilege extended by God which require responsible behavior.

In the parable of the Sower told by Jesus, his disciples cane to him privately and asked him about the parable. Jesus responded by saying, "To you it has been given to know the mystery of the kingdom of God; but to those who are outside, all things come in parables" (Mark 4:10, 11). In explaining the meaning of the parable Jesus asked; "Do you not understand this parable?" (Mark 4:13).

The disciples did not understand the meaning of the parable, even though as Jesus had previously said, it was given to them to understand. It was given to them to understand – speaking of privilege; but they did not understand – speaking of personal responsibility. The disciples did not understand the meaning of the parable possibly because they did not make proper use of the privilege extended to them to understand. Privilege must be matched with personal responsibility. However, Jesus extended grace to his disciples on account of their lack of understanding by explaining the parable to them. Like these early disciples, we often fall short in our effort to act perfectly in every situation and so God provide the means of grace as expressed through the city of refuge.

The negative effects of perfectionism are far reaching. Trying to live up to the unrealistic expectation of being perfect gives rise to unhappiness, frustration, and depression, because that which is earnestly sought after has always eluded the seeker. There is anxiety and guilt, arising from expecting to be the best at everything that we do. Our culture teaches that you must be the best because anything less is not good enough. Parents need to be the perfect parent, or they run the risk of having their child or children taken from them and given to others who are not perfect themselves. You must be extremely careful in everything you say and do and make sure that you do not offend anyone. However, we do at times offend one another. In fact, Jesus said to his disciples, "It is impossible that no offence should come" (Luke 17:1).

Unrealistic expectation for perfection is partly behind the use of performance enhancing drugs in sports, and in drug addiction in general – those who get hooked want to be always at their absolute best, because the society expect it of them, and only the best is good enough.

The unrealistic expectation for perfection is partly what forms the foundation, the drives and which legitimizes the frivolous lawsuits that are so common in our society. You are expected to be perfect at everything or you leave yourself open to lawsuits. In the secular world litigation is common for the simplest of infringement. "Florida woman is suing FedEx for tripping over a package left at her doorstep. . ... The lawsuit claims the deliveryman placed the package in the doorway of the home without properly notifying the woman of the delivery or of its close proximity to the door" (www.faceoflawsuitabuse.org). A seventy-nine-year-old woman filed a lawsuit against McDonalds and won, because she got burn from a cup of coffee she bought from McDonald, and which she accidentally spilled on herself (www.

en.wikipedia.org/wiki/Leibeck v. McDonald). In our culture, it is not enough to be extra careful, you must be perfect.

The unrealistic expectation for perfection is not much different for some in the church community. Little recognition and acknowledgment are given for work if it is not among the best.

Raymond Culpepper painted a picture of the unrealistic expectations of Pastor. The Ideal Pastor:

- Preaches 20 minutes and sits down.
- Condemns sin, but never hurts anyone's feelings.
- Works from 8 a.m. to 10 p.m. every day
- Does everything needed around the church, from preaching in the pulpit to unstopping the toilets.
- Is 26 years old and have been preaching for 30 years.
- Has a burning desire to work with teenagers and spend all his time with senior adults.
- Smiles all the time with a straight face because he has a sense of humor that keeps him seriously dedicated to his work.
- Makes 15 minutes calls each day and visits all his church members.
- Spends all his time evangelizing the unchurched.
- Is never away from the office or the phone (Preaching the Word, 2002, p. 141-142).

This description of the ideal pastor is quite humorous. However, this is what some individuals unconsciously expect of pastors. I have been serving in the pastoral ministry for over thirty (30) years. This has afforded me the opportunity to experience both extremes – those whose expectations of me are like the description above; and those who feel that as pastor there should be no greater expectation of me that than that expected from the average member of the congregation. Those who try to measure up to the description above will experience much disappointment and frustration and will only succeed in burning themselves out.

However, seeking to avoid the ills of perfectionism does not imply that one should not strive for excellence, which is a noble goal for life. One should seek to cultivate a healthy balance and understanding of both. The quest for excellence and the ills of perfectionism can be viewed as two sides of the same coin. While the former is a healthy pursuit of self-improvement, the latter is an unhealthy obsession with unattainable standards. Perfectionism may lead to anxiety and depression, while the pursuit of excellence can lead to personal growth and a sense of fulfillment. Perfectionism is an unattainable goal in this life, but the pursuit of excellence involves setting realistic goals and striving to achieve them. One should cultivate a growth mindset – embracing challenges, learning from mistakes, and seeing failures as opportunities for growth. By adopting a growth mindset, we can overcome the fear of failure that often accompanies perfectionism and focus on the process of learning and improving.

The apostle Paul in his letter to the Philippians discussed how he abandoned the pursuit of righteousness through the law (human efforts) which is unattainable, in pursuit a quality of righteousness which is "through faith in Christ, the righteousness which is from God by faith" (Philippians 3: 7-9). Paul acknowledged that he was not perfect. However, that did not prevent him from striving for a fuller experience with God. He said, "Not that I have already attained, or am already perfected; but I press on, that I may lay hold of that for which Christ Jesus has also laid hold of me. . .. I press toward the goal for the prize of the upward call of God in Christ Jesus" (Philippians 3:12- 14). While the quest for excellence is a noble pursuit, it is important to avoid falling into the trap of perfectionism. By recognizing the negative effects of perfectionism and cultivating a growth mindset, we can find balance and achieve our goals in a healthy and sustainable way.

The overly fascination with the spectacular at the expense of those things that lack glamor and flare is partly responsible for the lack of recognition given to some services even within the church community. In a discussion of the heroes of faith in (Hebrews chapter eleven), very rarely is acknowledgment and time given to those heroes who suffer for their faith. Heroes of faith that have their dead raised; those that escape the mouth of lions, and the fiery furnace will be highlighted. Rarely do we hear of the – "others were tortured, not accepting deliverance, that they might obtain a better resurrection. Still others had trial of mockings and scourgings, yes, and of the chains and imprisonment. They were stoned, they were sawn in two, were tempted, were slain with the sword. They wondered about in sheepskins and goatskins, being destitute, afflicted, tormented – of whom the world was not worthy. They wandered in deserts and mountains, in dens and caves of the earth. And all these, having obtained a good testimony through faith, did not receive the promise, God having provided something better for us, that they should not be made perfect apart from us" (Hebrews 11:35b-40).

When the work of successful pastors/leaders are discussed and recognized, rarely do the efforts of those who labor in/with small congregations in some difficult areas of society have their work associated with success. Success is associated with numbers, and not enough with faithfulness. While numbers are certainly a mark of success and should be emphasized, there are those who have been faithful in their small corners with the limited resources that they have available to them; they too are successful and should be recognized for their work. The work of those servants with ten talents, but so much the one with two talents. However, the Lord of those servants gave the same words of commendation to the servant that produced two other talents as he gave to the one that produced ten other talents. Following the flow of the parable, it is reasonable to assume that if the servant who had received one talent had worked on it, he would have received the same word of commendation as the other servants.

THE CITY OF REFUGE – GOD'S PROVISION FOR HUMAN WEAKNESS

In Paul's discussion on the gifts of the Spirit, he encouraged equal recognition and appreciation for all members of the body. Paul stated that "the body is one and has many members, but all the members of that one body, being many are one body, so also is Christ. . . And the eye cannot say to the hand, I have no need of you; nor again the head to the feet, I have no need of you. No, much rather, those members of the body which seem to be weaker are necessary. And those members of the body which we think to be less honorable, on these we bestow greater honor; and our unpresentable parts have greater modesty, but our presentable parts have no need. But God composed the body, having given greater honor to that part which lacks it, that there should be no schism in the body, but that the members should have the same care for one another. And if one member suffers, all the members suffer with it; or if one member is honored, all the members rejoice with it" (I Corinthians 12:12-26).

The point here is that there is also true value in the things that are not spectacular and glamorous, and less than perfect. Jesus had high praise for the poor widow who gave her two mites – "Truly I say to you that this poor widow has put in more than all; for all these out of their abundance have put in offerings for God, but she out of her poverty put in all the livelihood that she had" (Luke 21:3, 4). Our God values those who are less than perfect, and so he makes provision to help them to live.

The Lord's command to build cities of refuge is a divine provision for human weakness and failures due to imperfections. Implied in this command from the Lord to build cities of refuge for those who commit accidental and unintentional killing is that accidents will happen even among the people of God, and when they happen, they should be treated differently from when an act is done intentionally. Accidents are part of our lives; we try to avoid them, but they happen. Accidents are simply the natural results of imperfect people living in an imperfect world. The prophet Isaiah, having come to grips with his own imperfection in the awesome presence of the glory of God that he saw in a vision declared: "Woe is me for I am undone! Because I am a man of unclean lips, and I dwell in the midst of a people of unclean lips" (Isaiah 6:5). Human beings, and what they can achieve without the help of God is flawed.

The Lord is fully aware of man's inability to live perfectly, and so he made provisions for his shortcomings – Even without the command to build cities of refuge (Joshua 20:1-3), we see the principles of this command displayed in God's dealings with humanity after the fall. The spirit of the city of refuge was expressed early by God in his response to the failure of Adam and Eve after the fall. The first couple disobeyed the commands of the Lord, which resulted in them falling from fellowship with the Lord. They experienced shame, guilt, and fear, and went and hid themselves from the presence of God. To mask their nakedness, sin, and shame they used fig leaves to cover themselves. God went in search for them. He moved toward them even though they were the ones who had sinned against him. When he found them and enquired about them concerning their nakedness, Adam placed the blame for his disobedience and nakedness on Eve, and Eve placed it on the serpent. They both played the blame game instead of taking personal responsibility for their sinful action, and its subsequent consequence.

The Lord God punished Adam and Eve for their sin of disobedience. However, the Lord God did not stop there, he proceeded further to cover their nakedness – "Also for Adam and his wife the Lord God made tunics of skin and clothed them" (Genesis 3:21). The Lord God did not compromise his standard of holiness; neither did he make light of their sins, "the God of the earth did right." But he covered their nakedness, and in doing so, he made it possible for them to continue to live despite their sin and shame. The Lord God tempered justice with mercy.

The Lord made provision for the firstborn of the children of Israel to escape his judgment when he judged Egypt. He commanded them to kill a lamb and take some of its blood and put it of the doorposts and on the lintel of their houses where they eat the Passover lamb. "Now the blood shall be a sign for you on the houses where you are. And when I see the blood, I will pass over you" (Exodus 12:1ff.). The pascal lamb was a type of Christ – the spotless Lamb of God, who came and offered himself as a ransom for the sins of the world. When John the Baptist saw Jesus coming toward him, he said, "Behold! The lamb of God who takes away the sin of the world! (John 1:29). The firstborn of the children of Israel escaped the plague of the killing of the firstborn because of the mercy of God – the provision he made for safety.

I noticed in the Lord's dealing with Sarah regarding her lying about her laughing at the Lord's saying that she would bear a child in her old age. The Lord did not dwell on the fact that she lied, even though he did not condone her lying. He allowed her to know that he knew that she had laughed – "No, but you did laugh" (Genesis 18:15). However, his promise to her and Abraham was still in force. Jesus took a similar approach in his dealing with the woman caught in the act of adultery, and in his dealing with sinners in general. The law required that she be stoned to death. However, Jesus tempered justice with mercy – he gave her the opportunity to recover: "Neither do I condemn you, go and sin no more" (John 8:11).

Another Old Testament story that expresses the spirit of the city of refuge as God's provision for the failure of humanity is that recorded in the book of Hosea. God commanded Hosea to take a wife who was a harlot, and he took Gomer. She bore him children, but after a while she returned to her farmer life of harlotry. The Lord again commanded Hosea to go again and redeem her. "Then the LORD said to me, go again, love a woman who is loved by a lover and is committing adultery, just like the love of the LORD for the children of Israel, who took to other gods" (Hosea 3:1). All this was done to illustrate God's love and mercy for backsliding Israel.

We find a similar attitude displayed by Joseph in his dealing with what he thought was unfaithfulness on the part of Mary, his espoused wife. He sought to temper justice with mercy. Instead of disgracing her openly and condemning her to be put to death for the supposed unfaithfulness, we read, "Then Joseph her husband, being a just man, and not wanting to make her a public example, was mindful to put her away secretly" (Matthew 1:19).

These are examples of the principle of 'tempering justice with mercy' embedded in the function of the city of refuge, which makes provision of human failures or shortcomings. As people of faith, we must not compromise the truth of God's word or make light man's sinful behavior. However, we must find a way to hold justice and mercy in tension and temper justice with mercy. We must make provision for our own shortcomings and those of others, as the Lord did with the first couple. We must heed the command to build cities of refuge.

God's Provision for the Weakness and Imperfections of Humanity is also Expressed Through the Help/Assistance Given to the Slayer to Reach the City of Refuge

God's command to build cities of refuge, as his provision for man's shortcoming is further expressed through his command to provide easy access for the manslayer to escape to the city of refuge. The idea of easy access can be inferred from the number of cities of refuge, and their strategic position throughout the land so that wherever a man slayer was he would not be more than a day's journey from a city of refuge. The Lord also commands the children of Israel to prepare proper roads leading to the city of refuge, and that there be marked signposts on the roads pointing the way to the city of refuge. Merrill Unger stated that, "according to the rabbis, in order to aid the fugitive, it was the business of the Sanhedrin to keep the roads leading to the city of refuge in the best possible repair. No hills were left, every river was bridged, and the road itself was to be at least thirty-two cubits broad. At every turn where guideposts bearing the word 'Refuge,' and two students of the law were appointed to accompany the fleeing man and to pacify, if possible, the avenger, should he overtake the fugitive" (Unger, 2005, p. 240). All these provisions were to be made to give the slayer every opportunity to get to the city of refuge.

The manslayer had to exert some effort to escape – he had to run for his life. However, the probability of escaping was greatly heightened by the provisions that were made for him to escape. It is not enough to have opportunities of grace, there must also be reasonable access to such opportunities; and such accessibility should be available to everyone. The Lord commanded the children of Israel to make the cities of refuge available and accessible to the manslayer, whether he is an Israelite, a foreigner, or a sojourner. God is the God of the whole earth and is no respecter of persons.

God's provision for the manslayer to escape is of foremost importance. Because the presentation of the demands of God without the corresponding means of grace or provision for man's shortcomings is almost useless to a sinful imperfect creature. In fact, the Lord's righteous demands serve to lead us to Christ (see Romans 3:19, 20; Galatians 2:21). Through the righteous demands of God sinful man comes face to face with his wretchedness and his inability to save himself. However, John declared in his gospel that in the incarnation both grace and truth are revealed – "And the word became flesh, and dwelt among us, and we beheld his glory, glory as of the only begotten from the Father, **full of grace and truth**" (John 1:14). One should not be expressed at the expense of the other; it is not grace or truth but grace and truth. Ed Silvoso in his discussion of the biblical concepts of grace and truth (in John 1:14) in relation to sharing the gospel, said, "John lists grace and then truth to describe what he and others saw when they laid eyes on Jesus. First, they saw grace and then – and only then – they saw truth" . . . People do not feel attracted to our Jesus because before we talk about his love and compassion for sinners, we tend to emphasize his hatred of sin and the penalty unrepentant sinners must pay. And we do so with so much intensity that sinners have no option but to feel rejected" (Silvoso, 2000, P. 93, 95). What is advocated here is not even the presentation of grace before truth, but rather that they be presented together to be meaningful to fallen humanity.

The present discussion on asylum seekers to the United States by the two major political parties (republicans and democrats) is in a deadlock (stalemate). The republicans lay special emphasis on the law of the land – they make the point that many of those who are seeking asylum are breaking the law by entering the United States illegally. They are busy seeking all the options available to them to stop what they consider to be a part of illegal immigration. On the other hand, the democrats emphasized the fact that as a nation of immigrants we need to exercise greater understanding and help to those who are fleeing their homeland (which for them means poverty, pain, hardships and suffering of various forms) for to the United States, (which for them equate to a city of refuge). The arguments of both political parties on the subject are legitimate. However, by emphasizing one salient point at the expense of the other they have not helped the situation. The proper response is not either or - grace or truth, but rather both – grace and truth.

God's provision for the Weakness and Imperfections of His Creatures is Expressed Through the Protection Given to the Manslayer in the City of Refuge

The Lord gave the command that once the manslayer enters the city of refuge he should not be handed over to the avenger of blood without a trial; and once he has been proven innocent of the crime of murder he should be allowed to live within the walls of the city of refuge. While living in the city of refuge, the manslayer should not be treated as a prisoner, but as a bona fide resident – taking advantage of all the available privileges and benefits.

In our world today, many of those who have been accused of crimes and immoral behaviors are in a lot of instances tried in the media and other public sphere, and sometimes punished before there is ever a formal trial and the accused gets the opportunity to share his story. It happens at times before all the facts of the case are considered. At times innocence is established when all the facts of the case are presented. However, the damage has already been done- character has been damaged, and such individuals live with suspicion of wrongdoings hanging around their necks. Those who have failed, even after they have been punished for the wrongs that they have done, are deprived of some of the privileges that they need to recover and make good of their lives.

The church proclaims a message of grace, declaring to those we share the gospel with that the power of God can transform their lives, giving then the opportunities to live again. However, when some individuals respond positively to the gospel of grace and come to faith, they may not be allowed to serve in certain ministry areas because of their pass wrongs. The child molester who has served his time and was punished for his crime and who has repented of his sin is still not treated as a whole person. He is constantly reminded of his pass sin by the privileges and opportunities that are withheld. If such people go to the restroom, they are reminded; if they are seen talking with certain individuals they are reminded of their past. They are being treated as though the grace of God is powerless to effect positive change in their lives.

The born-again believer, who has repented of wrong doings, and has been transformed by the transforming power of God should not be treated like the murderer or as one who functions according to his farmer perversion but as one who is the beneficiary of the grace of God and is a new creation in God.

The risk of individuals who have failed to relapse to their farmer way of life is real, and therefore precautions should be taken. However, the fear of such taking place should not dictate the extent to which we involve such persons in ministry. If such a position is taken, then no one is qualified to serve. Some of us were brutes before we came to faith: some were liars, some were drug addicts, some were fornicators, robbers and thieves, and the list goes on. "If you, Lord, should mark iniquities, O Lord, who could stand? But there is forgiveness with you, that you may be feared" (Psalm 130:3). "But you were washed, but you were sanctified, but you were justified in the name of the Lord Jesus and by the Spirit of our God" (I Corinthians 6:11). We are who we are today only by the grace of God. God has forgiven us of our sins and has given us every opportunity to thrive. We must trust the grace of God in the lives of one another.

Having said that, the church is not oblivious of the challenge that individuals face in ridding themselves of past destructive sinful habits and addictive behaviors. Neither is it unaware of the law of the land regarding individuals who have committed certain crimes. However, our message of grace must be meaningful to all and must be more than proclamation in word, it must also include practice.

This is certainly not an easy task; and as was said before, the risk of things going wrong is real. However, we undermine the power of the grace of God to change the vilest of sinner when we continue to hold the past of individuals before them. True forgiveness involves making ourselves vulnerable again to those who have failed us. God himself trust us to do the right, we should trust others also. I have heard many individuals say, I forgive you, but I will not trust you again or make myself vulnerable to you again. To those who take this position, the Scripture admonishes, "and with the measure you use, it will be measured back to you" (Matthew 7:1, 2). What if the Lord should say to anyone of us after we have sought his forgiveness for some wrong; I forgive you, but I will not trust you again; or I forgive you, but I do not want to have anything more to do with you again. Let us practice the quality of forgiveness that we experience from the Lord.

The Lord treats those who have repented and runs to him for refuge as if they have never sinned. "The Lord is merciful and gracious, slow to anger, and abounding in mercy. He will not always strive with us, nor will he keep his anger forever. He has not dealt with us according to our sins, nor punished us according to our iniquities. For as the heavens are high above the earth, so great is his mercy toward those who fear him; as far as the east is from the west, so far has he removed our transgressions from us" (Psalm 103:8-12).

The City of Refuge Communicates Divine Privilege and Advocates Personal Responsibility – "appoint for yourself cities of refuge" (Joshua 20:2)

The Children of Israel were commanded to build cities of refuge in the Promised Land for themselves, and not simply for some heathen nations around. This implies that the time will come when they need it. God made the Provision by issuing the command to build a place of refuge; man has the Responsibility to build it. The command to build city of refuge is a divine privilege that God extended to fallen humanity. God sees our pain and suffering because of our weaknesses and vulnerability, and he offer us a means to cope.

However, we need to make proper use of this divine privilege, we must build cities of refuge for ourselves. Paul's word to the Philippian church is applicable here. Paul said, "work out your own salvation with fear and trembling; for it is God who works in you both to will and to do for his good pleasure" (Philippians 2:12, 13). God has made the provision and has given us the means to succeed. Now we must take advantage of such privilege that God provides and work it out in our daily lives. To escape from the avenger of blood, and the inevitable pressures of life, you must build cities of refuge, and when the need arises you must run into them.

We must acknowledge that we have fallen short of God's glory; that we are imperfect and in need of the protection of God, because we cannot live without it. We can only go so far without the cities of refuge. It will only be a matter of time until we all need such a place of protection. We sometimes fail to build cities of refuge because we are either not aware of our own vulnerability or we are not humble enough to admit our need for it. We deceive ourselves into believing that we can make it on our own.

When you seek to protect the innocent, you are protecting yourself also. When you see to the needs of others you are in effect making provision for your own needs. You protect yourself from becoming callous, heartless, and revengeful. When you build a city of refuge you are guarding against your own weaknesses and making provision for your own safety when the need arises. Jesus told the parable of the unjust steward, who was commended for acting shrewdly in making provision for when he would be out of a Job (see Luke 16:1- 8). When you build you are building for yourself.

Like the Good Samaritan, we should exercise compassion for others in their need because such is the right thing to do, and we are on the same road of life. What has happened to others can happen to us save for the grace of God. Paul also speaks about this issue of showing concern for others in need. He said, "Brethren, if a man is overtaken in any trespass, you who are spiritual restore such a one in a spirit of gentleness, considering yourself lest you also be tempted. Bear one another's burdens, and so fulfill the law of Christ" (Galatians 6:1, 2). When you exercise mercy toward others in their pain, you inevitably open the door for mercy to be shown to you when you are in need. Jesus said, "blessed are the merciful, for they shall obtain mercy" (Matthew 5:7). You are in effect building for yourself cities of refuge.

You need to build cities of refuge for yourself before you have need of it. Because you may not have the time or the where with all to build it when you need it. In the parable of the ten virgins, the five wise ones took oil with them. However, the five foolish ones took their lamps but took no oil with them. When the midnight cry was uttered, "Behold, the bridegroom is coming; go out to meet him". The wise virgins were ready to go because they took oil with them. However, the foolish ones were locked out because they did not take the time to properly prepare themselves, when they had the opportunity to do so. The wise built before they needed it, but the foolish ones did not. Build it before you need it.

The city of refuge was made available to the fugitive, but he had to run into it for safety. This implies urgency. Urgency in escaping the avenger who was hotly pursuing him. Urgency in turning away from the sinful practices that cause him to be in the position that he was in before they destroy him. The account of the escape of Lot, his wife and his two daughters from Sodom illustrate such urgency that a slayer should take in his escape. It stated: "When the morning dawned, the angels urged Lot to hurry, saying, arise, take your wife and your two daughters who are here, lest you be consumed in the punishment of the city. And while he lingered, the men took hold of his hand, his wife's hand, and the hands of his two daughters, the Lord being merciful to him. . . when they had brought them outside, that he said, escape for your life! Do not look behind you nor stay anywhere in the plain. Escape to the mountains, least you be destroyed" (Genesis 19:15-17). The responsibility to create cities of refuge must be taken by the people of God. It must not be taken lightly or be left undone.

The City of Refuge: A Place of Safety that is Conducive to Self-Disclosure

When the manslayer runs to the city of refuge, he shall find sanctuary there: "And when he flees to one of those cities and stand at the entrance of the gate of the city and declares his case in the hearing of the elders of that city, they shall take him into the city as one of them, and give him a place, that he may dwell among them. Then if the avenger of blood pursues him, they shall not deliver the slayer into his hand.. .... And he shall dwell in that city until he stands before the congregation for judgment" (Joshua 20:4-6).

The city of refuge is a safe place. Such a place that is welcoming, and where there is no fear of danger facilitates self-disclosure and encourages the slayer to come clean. A place to refresh and revive from the stressful and demanding conditions of life. Cities city of refuge are safe places that provide opportunities not only for rest and relaxation from the physical, mental, and emotional draining conditions, but also from time of spiritual low. Safe places that provide opportunities for introspection and meditation. Rest from the busyness of activities, information overload; unrealistic expectation, and other conditions that are physically, spiritually, and emotionally draining. Jesus acknowledged and stressed the importance of this, when he said to his disciples, after a successful mission trip, "come aside and rest awhile" (Mark 6:31). Cleland Bo yd McAfee 1903 hymn said it well, "There is a place of quiet rest, near to the heart of God; a place where sin cannot molest, near to the heart of God. There is a place of comfort sweet, near to the heart of God. A place where we our Savior meet, near to the heart of God."

The manslayer knows that once he enters the city of refuge, he will be safe from all harm until he is given a fair trial. The avenger may pursue him, and may hurl accusations and insults at him, but the slayer is assured that once he makes it to the city of refuge he will not be handed over to the slayer unless he is tried and found guilty. "He who dwells in the secret place of the Most High shall abide under the shadow of the Almighty. I will say of the Lord, he is my refuge and my fortress; my God, in him I will trust" (Psalm 91:1, 2). The city of refuge is therefore a place of safety that facilitates and encourages self-disclosure.

City of refuge – A Place Where One Will Be Treated Fairly and With Grace

The city of refuge served as a means of offering protection and fairness in a time when retribution and vengeance were prevalent. Within the city of refuge, the slayer was treated fairly and with grace. He was granted asylum and provided with the opportunity to present his case and share his story before the city elders and authorities. There the slayer will be listened to with ears and hearts of understanding, compassion and with empathy, and not with an attitude of condemnation. If his actions were deemed to be truly unintentional, he would be granted refuge, and would be protected from harm if he remained within the city's borders. This concept reflects the commitment of the principle of justice tempered with mercy, a hallmark of the Judeo-Christian tradition.

The city of refuge concept goes beyond simple protection; it embodies the biblical values of grace, forgiveness, and the acknowledgement that not all wrongdoing is intentional. It also emphasized the importance of due process and a fair trial, ensuring that hasty and impulsive acts did not lead to unnecessary suffering or bloodshed. This biblical concept served as a beacon of compassion and a reminder of the importance of fairness and forgiveness in the pursuit of Justice. What is being expressed in the city of refuge is not sloppy justice, or miscarriage of justice or lack of accountability, but humanness, empathy, and forgiveness. Such an attitude of grace and fair play encourages self-disclosure.

In today's world, the city of refuge concept can be seen as a timeless reminder of the value and necessity of grace, forgiveness, and the need for a justice system that seeks to balance retribution with compassion. It emphasizes the importance of recognizing unintentional harm and providing a safe place for individuals to make amends and seek reconciliation, ultimately promoting a more just and compassionate society.

City of Refuge – A 'Safe Place' that is Conducive to Self-disclosure and the Willingness to Come Clean

The scripture teaches that "Whoever conceals his transgressions will not prosper, but he who confesses and forsakes them will obtain mercy" (Proverbs 28:13 ESV). And again, "If we say we have no sin, we deceive ourselves, and the truth is not in us. If we confess our sins, he is faithful and just to forgive us our sins and to cleanse us from all unrighteousness" (I John 1:8, 9). These passages make clear the point that those who acknowledge and own up to their sins will be shown mercy. Many individuals among us are secretly experiencing pain and are suffering physically, emotionally, spiritually/psychologically, socially, and otherwise, because of unconfessed sins. However, many of these individuals find it extremely hard/difficult to self-disclose, even though coming clean is the right thing to do.

In the text: *Secret Keeping: Overcoming Hidden Habits and Addictions.* Prin, the author of the text, outlined the necessary steps to be taken on the road to recovery from such behaviors. This includes a decision to surrender the secret keeping behaviors, and to seek help to do so; doing a careful and honest introspection of the self and the nature of the addictive behavior and accept it for what it is; prepare to state the true facts; disclose the true facts; trust in a new worldview; and account for present and future behaviors. He suggested that disclosure should flow from the self to God, then to some professional (counselor, therapist, clergy, etc.), and then to the ones that are most affected by the secretive behaviors (Prin, September 2006, p. 168-169).

Prin, like many others, advocates full disclosure of harmful secret behaviors as a necessary component for healing to take place for both the secret keeper and those hurt by his/her harmful behaviors. Although disclosing harmful behaviors can be incredibly stressful and painful for all involved, it nonetheless brings healing.

Those who disclose secret harmful behaviors reported feeling better when they do and feel that disclosure was the right thing to do.

However, it is no secret that many individuals who do terrible things or individuals who practice harmful behaviors do not come clean. They do not own up to these wrongs and seek help to recover. While some of these individuals do not come clean because of rebellion and the wickedness of their hearts, there are others who struggle to come clean out of fear that coming clean will yield no positive in their lives but will put them in a worst position. Upon reflection, there seem to be some other factors that greatly influence disclosure of secrets sinful behaviors and coming clean: the creating of or presence of a 'safe place' to self-disclose, and that of providing hope or a future for those who self-disclose – tempering justice with mercy.

The presence of a 'safe place' that is conducive to the disclosure of behaviors that are in some cases potentially damming, and which may result in unbearable embarrassment is paramount. 'Safe places' lessens the pain associated with the act of disclosure and heightens the probability for healing. The average person finds it much easier to self-disclose to the Lord because his presence is welcoming, and he does not use the information to destroy. Rather, when from our heart we confess and forsake our evil ways, the Lord forgives and helps us to overcome.

King Ahab and king Manasseh are two of the evilest kings that rule over the children of Israel – Ahab over the northern kingdom of Israel, and Manasseh over the kingdom of Judah (see I Kings 16:29 – 34; 21:25, 26; 2 Kings 21:1-12). However, they both repented of their evil ways and were forgiven (see I Kings 21:27-29; 2 Chronicles 33:10ff.). The parable of the prodigal son beautifully illustrates the blessings that follow repentance (coming clean). Luke gave the prodigal son's confession and his compassionate father's response: "And the son said to him, father, I have sinned against heaven and in your sight, and am no longer worthy to be called your son. But the father said to his servants, bring out the best robe and put it on him and put a ring on his hand and sandals on his feet. And bring the fatted calf here and kill it and let us eat and be merry; for this my son was dead and is alive again; he was lost and is found. And they began to be merry" (Luke15:21-24).

Providing hope or a future for those who own up to their wrongs is also critical for self-disclosure – "whoever confesses and forsakes them will have mercy", and "If we confess our sins, he is faithful and just to forgive us our sins, and to cleanse us from all unrighteousness" (Proverbs 28:13b; I john 1:9). Ahab, Manasseh, and the prodigal son all owned up to their sins and were all forgiven. While not making big promises that things will be well when disclosure takes place, there is nonetheless a need to give hope to those involved. Individuals who see no hope in coming clean will likely find it exceedingly difficult to do so; while those who are given reason to hope will be more inclined to come clean.

This can be done if real opportunities are provided for individuals who come clean to be readjusted in society and go on to make some good of their lives (after paying the price for their harmful behaviors). The bleak future that lies ahead of some offenders make the process of self-disclosure difficult, and relapse into the harmful behaviors more likely. The child abuser faces jail time, shame, and disgrace, to loved ones, and the label of a sex offender for almost all his/her life; the unfaithful or abusive spouse faces divorce, shame and loss of fellowship with family members and friends; the failing pastor or professional faces losing his/her professional license and the privilege to practice his/her chosen profession, and possibly public shame and disgrace, and the list goes on. In other words, the result of disclosure may cause such pain and suffering, the magnitude of which may blur any motivation to come clean.

In April 2007 CNN reporters John Zarrella and Patrick Oppmann reported a story concerning the plight of sex offenders in the state of Florida. Highlights of the story posted on the internet read, "sex offenders cannot live within 2,500 feet of places children might gather. In an urban area like Miami, this leaves few options for the convicted criminals; a handful of sex offenders are now living under a bridge." When the difficulty of getting a job, the fact that the names of sex offenders are made known whenever they move into any area, among other challenges are added to such hash living conditions, it becomes that more difficult for persons who are engaged in such behaviors to disclose and come clean. The tension created by having to choose between the pain experienced from remaining in secretive behavior, and the pain associated with disclosure, is what I believe is a major factor that will determine the path taken.

The Lord invites sinful man to come clean, but he also offers hope when he does – "Come, now, and let us reason together, says the Lord, though your sins are like scarlet, they will be as white as snow; though they are red like crimson, they shall be like wool. If you are willing and obedient, you shall eat the good of the land" (Isaiah 1:18, 19). To encourage disclosure among secret keepers who are engaged in harmful behaviors, it is vital to create a 'safe place' and present meaningful opportunity for readjustment and personal growth after disclosure. The city of refuge is that place where individuals can experience both and expect some means of grace.

The City of Refuge - A Place of Rest, Restoration, and Rediscovery of God (his Presence, Purpose, and Power), and the Self

When the slayer enters the city of refuge and having convinced the congregation that his or her action that resulted in the death to another person and caused grief and pain to the loved ones that are related to the deceased was an accident, and was unintentional, and he is allowed to live in the city of refuge, the slayer enters a period of rest, restoration, and rediscovery of God and the self. The "City of Refuge" provides rest and relaxation from the physical, mental, spiritual, and emotional draining conditions resulting from the death his action caused. Realizing the pain caused to someone can be a profound source of internal suffering, leading to sleepless nights, anxiety and even depression. Guilt and remorse can weigh heavily on the conscience of the slayer. There is the struggle with such thoughts as – could I have avoided the accident? Was there anything that could have been done differently? Was the accident his fault? The stigma attached to being labeled a manslayer can be a heavy cross to bear.

The slayer also may have to grapple with the feeling that he may have damaged his own life as well; ruined relationships, lost opportunities and tarnished his reputation. These and other concerns can have a devastating effect on the slayer. However, being in the city of refuge provides an opportunity for the slayer to heal from these and other struggles and pain and find hope to live again. The slayer knows that the avenger cannot pursue him there, and so he can rest from the stress resulting from such fear. He can rest from running and concentrate his effort on reconnecting with God and the self. He can reconnect with God as the one who has the power to forgive, and who is willing to do so. He can reconnect with God who is a very present help in trouble. He can reconnect with God's will and purpose for his life.

Being in the city of refuge, away from the business of life on the outside, provides ample time for personal reflection and introspection. It affords time to be with yourself and to get to know yourself better – your strengths and weaknesses; your successes and your failures; obstacles and opportunities, and above all the hope and grace that is available to you in God. It also provides time to practice *lectio divina,* (the Latin for divine reading). This is a traditional monastic practice that involves the slow reading of the scriptures, meditating on what was read, praying, and contemplating. This practice promote communion with God, and the rediscovery of the joy of living and being in the presence of God.

THE CITY OF REFUGE - GOD'S PROVISION FOR HUMAN WEAKNESS

I recall in my early Christian life while living in the island of Jamaica. I would use the greater part of my lunch time at my job to go into the nearby bushes to read the word of God, meditate and pray. I would engage in this practice at least three times per week. Such activity helped me to practice entertaining the presence of God and get to know the Lord through his word. These spiritual exercises also prepared me to face and overcome the text and challenges of life.

Sometimes during the mad rush of the day and even engagement in ministry activities, it is extremely easy to lack fellowship, communion, and time away with God to recharge for the journey ahead. Being in the "City of Refuge" affords for quality time and communion with God, which facilitates the rediscovery of the presence, purpose, and power of God. The chorus of the popular worship song said it well: "Shut in with God in a secret place; there in the Spirit beholding his face; gaining more power to run in the race, I love to be shut in with God."

CHAPTER 4

THE CITY OF REFUGE – GOD'S PROVISION OF GRACE IN CHRIST

The idea of the city of refuge which provides grace to those who have failed along the way is taken to its highest level in Christ Jesus. Jesus is God's ultimate means of grace for fallen humanity – he is the true city of refuge. "Nor is there salvation in any other, for there is no other name under heaven given among men by which we must be saved" (Acts 4:12). He is the true city of refuge to which we all must run to escape the righteous judgment of God. All who came before the incarnation look forward to him and all who will come after the incarnation look back to Jesus. He is the ultimate priest who once and for all offers himself as the ultimate sacrifice. "And every priest stands ministering daily and offering repeatedly the same sacrifices, which can never take away sins. But this man, after he had offered one sacrifice for sins forever, sat down at the right hand of God, from that time waiting till his enemies are made his footstool. For by one offering he has perfected forever those who are being saved" (Hebrews 10:11-14).

Christ as God's final city of refuge goes far beyond that presented in the old covenant. In fact, the principles present in the Old Testament teachings on the city of refuge all looked forward to

Christ, who is the ultimate fulfillment of them all. Boice cited the following spiritual parallels relative to Christ being our city of refuge: "it was the duty of the Jews to clearly indicate the way to the cities of refuge. . . This is a good parallel to our responsibility to make the way to Christ easily accessible to the lost. . . . The gates to these cities were always to be open, just as the arms of Christ are always open to receive any who come to him. . . . The cities of refuge was not only for Jews but for people of all races. Similarly, the salvation available in Jesus Christ is for all. . . If an ancient manslayer did not flee to one of the cities of refuge, there was no hope for him; there was no other provision in the Law of Israel in which he might be saved. . . . There is only one way: Jesus. You must flee to him" (Boice, 2006, p. 111-112).

Under the old covenant, the death of the high priest who was serving at the time the slayer entered the city of refuge would free the slayer to return to public life in the general community. The slayer need not fear death at the hand of the avenger anymore. Jesus our great high priest is the author of a better covenant. His death releases all humanity who put their faith in him and run to him for refuge. For "inasmuch then as the children have partaken of flesh and blood, he himself likewise shared in the same, that through death he might destroy him who had the power over death, that is, the devil, and release those who through fear of death were all their lifetime subject to bondage" (Hebrews 2:14, 15).

The death of the high priest under the old covenant releases the slayer to return to public life, but it was powerless to take away sin or free him from a guilty conscience. However, Jesus' death not only release those who put faith in him from death, but his death also cleanses the fugitive of sin and of a guilty conscience (see Hebrews 9: 11-14; 10:1-10). The freedom that the fugitive gained through the death of the high priest was temporary and incomplete because the slayer later died. But by the death of our great High priest, Jesus, we are saved to the uttermost (Hebrews 7:25; 9:12). Whereas the high priests under the old covenant was seized by death, and such death brought freedom to the fugitive. Jesus laid down his life freely for us – "for this he did once for all when he offered up himself" (Hebrews 7:27b; 9:13, 15-28; 10:10-14). Jesus is the author of a better covenant. The earthly priesthood was a shadow and copy of the heavenly (8:5).

In the account of the saving of Noah and his family from the great flood and the saving of the firstborn of Israel during the plagues of Egypt. There was no other means of salvation save that which the Lord provided. Likewise, there is no other means of salvation apart from Jesus – "Nor is there salvation in any other, for there is no other name given among men by which we must be saved" (Acts 4:12). Jesus is God's appointed way of salvation. He is the lamb, slain before the foundation of the world; the lamb that takes away the sins of the world.

Despite these spiritual parallels there is a striking difference between the law of the city of refuge in the Old Testament, and that of Jesus God's ultimate city of refuge. Whereas those who were welcomed in the city of refuge were innocent of intentional sin, and those who committed premeditated murders were not welcomed; all those who find refuge in Christ Jesus are guilty before God – "for all have sinned and fall short of the glory of God." "For when we were still without strength, in due time Christ died for the ungodly. For scarcely for a righteous man will one die; yet perhaps for a good man someone would even dare to die. But God demonstrates his love toward us, in that while we were still sinners, Christ died for us" (Romans 3:23; 5:6-8). "For Christ also suffered once for sins, the just for the unjust, that he might bring us to God" (I Peter 3:18). Christ Jesus died in our stead, as well as for us that we might live through him. Once a sinner acknowledges his sin, confesses it, and seeks refuge in Christ Jesus, he shall be saved. "If we confess our sins, he is faithful and just to forgive us our sins and to cleanse us from all unrighteousness" (I John 1:9).

David is a prime example that there is forgiveness for those guilty of premeditated killing. David committed adultery with Bathsheba,

Uriah's wife. When he discovered that she was pregnant, he tried to conceal his sin by trying to get Uriah to go home to sleep with his wife, but Uriah would not (see 2 Samuel 11:11). After several unsuccessful attempts to get Uriah to go home, David devised a plan to have Uriah killed. He drafted the plan and sent it by the hand of Uriah to Joab, the commander of the army. After the death of Uriah, the prophet Nathan confronted David concerning his sin. David acknowledged his sin and repented, and the Lord God forgave him (see Psalm 51).

In Christ there is no condemnation. In Christ Jesus both those who are innocent of intentional killing and those who are guilty, can find refuge in Jesus if they run to him. Jesus declared,

"Come to me, all you who labor and are heavy laden, and I will give you rest. Take my yoke upon you and learn from me, for I am gentle and lowly in heart, and you will find rest for your souls" (Matthew 11:28, 29). Like the compassionate father in the parable of the Prodigal Son, Jesus will receive anyone who will come to him. "For we do not have a High Priest who cannot sympathize with our weaknesses, but was in all points tempted as we are, yet without sin. Let us therefore come boldly to the throne of grace, that we may obtain mercy and find grace to help in our time of need" (Hebrews 4:15, 16).

Considering that we have a High Priest who is willing and able to help us in our time of need, how them must we live? We must run to him and take refuge in him, for he is willing and able to save us, and he is our only hope for survival. Through Christ Jesus we are not only able to escape from the enemy of our souls, but we will find strength to live the life that is pleasing to God. Through Christ Jesus we are not only prepared for this present life, but for the life to come.

Taking advantage of live through Christ Jesus means believing in him for your salvation. This is not simply a matter of intellectual assent. Neither is it simply to be fully persuaded about who he is and what he can do for you. Rather, it is to put confidence in him for your eternal salvation, and not trust in your ability to save yourself through your good works.

The story was told of a man who was trained to walk and push a wheelbarrow on a rope tied across a water falls. A crowd gathered, everyone wanting to go across the fall but crossing on the rope was the only way. The man trained to walk across the fall on the rope asked, which of you believe that I can walk across the falls on the rope? Everyone responded in the affirmative because they knew that he was thus trained. Which of you believe that I can take someone in a wheelbarrow across? Again, everyone answered in the affirmative. Then he asked one final question, who will be the first to sit in the wheelbarrow and allow me to take you across? No one was willing to go forward. To do so would mean putting your life in the hand of the man. Likewise, trusting Jesus means to stake your eternal destiny in the hand of God.

Secondly, taking advantage of life through Jesus involves living out the new life in Christ Jesus in your daily lives make practical the life of Christ – "For if any man be in Christ, he is a new creation. Loving others as Christ have loved you – (John 3:16; I John 3:16); showing mercy to others as you have received; and forgiving others as God for Christ's sake has forgiven you.

Lastly, appropriating the life of Christ also involve proclaiming it in word and in deed. Jesus not only preach deliverance from sin, but he also involves himself in dealing with the various malady resulting from sin – healing the sick, feeding the hungry, etc. A missionary went into a remote area where the villagers never hear about Jesus. He lived among them for several years and then he died without preaching about Jesus. Years later, a group of missionaries went into the same area and began to talk about Jesus and all the good thing that he did. The villagers responded, "We know that person of whom you speak, he once lived here among us.' The first missionary had so modeled the life of Christ that the villagers thought he was that person. We are to so live our lives that others will see Christ through us and glorify God. We are called to be a witness, and to do witnessing.

CHAPTER 5

CITY OF REFUGE – THE CHURCH AS A CITY OF REFUGE

Arguments From the Nature of the Church

Our world in general as well as our churches are filled with wounded people. People who have tried and have failed because of their own weaknesses and inability to cope with the challenges of life; people who have failed because they do not have the skill sets that they need to succeed, and they fail in their effort to acquire them. Then there are those who are wounded from self-esteem and self-image that have been damaged and marred during early childhood, and the effect of such have affected them far into their adult life, because such situations have never been addressed or sufficiently addressed. There are also individuals who are wounded because they have failed, and they desire a second chance which they never had. People who were born with emotional, physical, and mental defects, and from which they never got the help they need to experience some degree of wholeness so they can achieve some measure of success with their disabilities. People who are wounded because of the lack of compassion shown to them in their struggles, toils, and distresses in life.

It was said of Jesus during his earthly ministry:

> *Then Jesus went about all the cities and villages, teaching in their synagogues, preaching the gospel of the kingdom and healing every sickness and every disease among the people. But when he saw the multitudes, he was moved with compassion for them because they were weary and scattered, like sheep having no shepherd. Then he said to his disciples, the harvest truly is plentiful, but the laborers are few. Therefore, pray to the Lord of the harvest to send out laborers into his harvest (Matthew 9:35-38).*

In response to these conditions of suffering some members of the witnessing community have at times focused most of their efforts on winning the lost and pointing them to the age to come when conditions will be better. Others have directed most of their attention and limited resources in addressing these and other social needs at the expense of the proclamation of the gospel. However, the church community must recognize the validity of both evangelism and social action as integral parts of the proclamation of the gospel and its Christian ministry. The gospel needs to be proclaimed in word and deed. The church must find a way of integrating these two vital components of Christian mission into one holistic ministry without compromising either one. Jesus would have his followers to model his approach to ministry and minister to the suffering ones among them.

The church is described in scripture as the body of Christ, and as the temple of God among other designations. "For we have many members in one body, but all the members do not have the same function, so we, being many, are one body in Christ" (Romans 12:4, 5); "And he put all things under his feet, and gave him to be head over all things to the church, which is his body, the fulness of him who fills all in all" (Ephesians 1:22, 23). As the body of Christ, the church is Christ representative in the earth. Paul declared:

"Now all things are of God who has reconciled us to himself through Jesus Christ, and has given us the ministry of reconciliation, that is, that God was in Christ reconciling the world to himself, not imputing their trespasses to them, and has given to us the word of reconciliation. Now then, we are ambassadors for Christ as though God were pleading through us, be reconciled to God" (2 Corinthians 5:18-20). While Jesus was here in the flesh, he declared himself to be his Father's representative in the earth (text). Just before he ascended to the Father he said to his disciples, "As the Father has sent me, I also send you" (John 20:21). The church as sent into the world by Christ continues the mission that Christ was engaged in. The statement "as the father has sent me, so I am sending you" signaled that Jesus' mission on earth has been completed. However, the same mission continues through the church. While Jesus was on earth he ministered to the "poor" and disenfranchised of his day. He healed the sick, comforted the oppressed and the depressed, he invited the weary to come to him so that they could find and enjoy rest in him, he gave hope to the hopeless, and forgave the sins of those who came to him. As the body of Christ, the church must also minister to the needs of those who have failed and need hope and a place of refuge. This is the calling and purpose of the church. In carrying out this mission, the church must be faithful to the trust committed to it and be relevant to the context in which it ministers.

During Jesus' earthly ministry he proclaimed himself to be the light of the world. As His representative on the earth, the church is now described as the salt of the earth and the light of the world. It must proclaim the light of the gospel in word, deed and wonder for all to see. Jesus said to his early disciples, "You have not chosen me, but I chose you and appointed you that you should go and bear fruit, and that your fruit should remain, that whatever you ask the father in my name, he may give you" (John 15:16).

THE CITY OF REFUGE

The Law of the Land and the Practices of the Church

The legal system of the United States, as in other parts of the world has caused undue pain and suffering in the lives of numerous individuals who have used drugs and engaged in other illegal and criminal activities, by keeping their criminal records for all to see, even after they have paid the price for their wrongdoings and served the sentences commuted to them by the law of the land. This condition affects these individuals in several areas of their lives. They find it difficult to get jobs or good paying jobs, to get loans from financial institutions, to make use of the opportunities for education, find suitable places to live, and to make proper use of other situations in which a background check is necessary. In most cases, these individuals are not befriended by the elites of society or by those who can have a positive influence on their lives. They often must find friends and companions among those who are in a comparable situation to theirs, and who are in no position to offer meaningful help. This heightens the possibility of them relapsing into their farmer life of crime.

Calls have been made for criminal justice reform that includes the expunging of the criminal records of some criminals (seal them from public view, remove them from databases, and neutralize most of the legal effects). Particularly of those criminals who have paid their dues to society for their wrongdoings and are consciously trying to reform themselves. Such reform of the criminal justice system would go a far way in giving them a second chance to make something good of their lives and have a good chance to survive. Keeping their criminal records after they have paid the price for their wrongs has crippled the lives of so many and has made it extremely difficult for such individuals to recover from their failures and setbacks and move on to live successful lives.

The Pennsylvania General Assembly has acknowledged to some degree some of these concerns. In their General Assembly 2018 Act 56, the following is declared among other concerns:

(1). Individuals with charges not leading to convictions may be inherently harmed by the maintenance of that record and have a constitutional presumption of innocence.
(2). After less violent individuals convicted of crimes have served their sentences and remained crime free long enough to demonstrate rehabilitation, the individuals' access to employment, housing, education, and other necessities of life should be fully restored.
(3). The Commonwealth shall provide a clean slate remedy, as set forth under this act, to:
  (i). Create a strong incentive for avoidance of recidivism by offenders.
  (ii). Provide hope for the alleviation of the hardships of having a criminal record by offenders who are trying to rehabilitate themselves.
  (iii). Save the Commonwealth money that must be spent in the administration of criminal justice when offenders recidivate.
  (iv). Ensure appropriate access to criminal history information by criminal justice agencies.
(4). The clean slate remedy should be implemented without cost to the former offender of filing a petition with a court.

Although limited expungement is available for some individuals who have committed certain crimes, many of such Individuals do not have such information regarding the process to follow to have their criminal records expunged; while some of those who do, do not have the resources to access such privileges. They continue to live their lives with the shame and guilt of their past hanging around their necks. In response to such a call for criminal justice reform, some states like the Commonwealth of Pennsylvania have made some adjustment to their laws to ease the pain that some individuals are experiencing. However, much more needs to be done if meaningful change is to be realized.

The Tension Between the Law of the Land and the Mission of the Church

The church promulgates a theology of forgiveness. The tenets of this theology often stand in tension with the demands of the law. It is a fact that when some individuals have served their sentences for their crimes, they are not allowed to function as normal members of the general society as well as of the faith community even after repenting of their sins and accepting the Lord Jesus as their personal Lord and Savior. Child abusers who have paid for their crimes, repented of their sins, and have demonstrated genuine transformation of their lives are not allowed to work with children. The church proclaims a message of the power of the gospel to transform lives but has in effect put some of these conditions beyond the power of the gospel to transform, by still holding up some individuals' past before them. By not allowing individuals who have repented of their sins of abuse and other crimes and have been faithfully following the Lord to function as 'normal' believers, the church has undermined the power of the gospel to transform some people's lives, and the message of grace that it preaches.

While not being oblivious of the challenge that these and other individuals face in ridding themselves of past destructive and sinful behaviors; and while being aware of the law of the land regarding individuals who have committed certain crimes; and while proper care must be taken in engaging these individuals in some areas of ministry, and while accountability and discipleship is of utmost importance for those who have committed such crimes as child abuse before and during their involvement in ministry with children, our message of grace must be available to all and must be more than proclamation, it must also involve practice. What is proclaimed in words must be practiced in our daily lives or the message of the power of the gospel to transform the lives of the vilest of sinner will be undermined.

Jesus in response to this situation, declared that he came to address these and other ills of humanity. He said, "The Spirit of the Lord is upon me, because he has anointed me to preach the gospel to the poor; he has sent me to heal the broken hearted, to proclaim liberty to the captives and the recovery of sight to the blind, to set at liberty those who are oppressed; to proclaim the acceptable year of the Lord" (Luke 4:18, 19). The "poor" of our world not only refers to those who lack the basic material things in life – food, clothing, shelter, and other basic amenities of life. The poor also refers to those who are spiritually, morally, and emotionally bankrupt; those who are physically and mentally challenged to the point that they are unable to properly care for themselves; those who possess the physical amenities of life but are lonely, lacking companionship or individuals that they can call their friends. Then there are those who lack hope and the will to live; and those who lack the skills and abilities to responsibly manage the challenges of life, and therefore are going through life without any real sense or feeling of accomplishment, satisfaction and meaning to their lives. Jesus was the most effective teacher and proclaimer of the word because he fully embodies the message he preaches. He was not afraid to go against the accepted norm of society when such runs contrary to the message he proclaimed.

Jesus, during his earthly ministry demonstrated concern for the "poor." In the story of the woman caught in the act of adultery, Jesus said to her, "Neither do I condemn you; go and sin no more" (John 8:11). To the Samaritan woman at the well at Sychar, who had five failed marriages, Jesus showed compassion on her, and she carried the gospel to her country men (John 4:5-30). In his dialogue with Zacchaeus the tax collector, Jesus said, "Today salvation has come to this house, because he also is a son of Abraham; for the Son of Man has come to seek and to save that which was lost" Luke 19:9, 10). Jesus allowed a woman described as a sinner by the Pharisees to wash his feet with her tears, wiped them with her hair, and anoint them with the fragrant oil (Luke 7:36-39); Jesus after his resurrection, appeared first to Mary Magdalene (our of whom he cast out seven devils) and commissioned her to take the message of his resurrection to the rest of his disciples (John 20:11-17). It is further said of Jesus, "For we do not have a High Priest who cannot sympathize with our weaknesses, but was in all points tempted as we are, yet without sin. Let us therefore come boldly to the throne of grace, that we may obtain mercy and find grace to help in a time of need" (Hebrews 4:15, 16).

Jesus commissioned his followers to continue the mission of God in which he was engaged. He said to his disciples, "As the Father has sent me, I also send you" (John 20:21). The church is that body of individuals that must continue the mission of God to a wounded, hopeless and dying world. Ministering to those who have failed is at the heart of the gospel. The church must find ways to provide healing and hope for those who have failed – the church needs to be a city of refuge for the oppressed.

However, although the church ought to be a place of refuge for those who have failed and are failing, the church is considered by some within the church community to be a community comprising only of mature and whole people. Many within the church community have little tolerance for wounded people resulting from their failures. McMahan posited that, "Today's church only sees itself as consisting of successful people, and its tolerance for failure is low. Its desire and passion are not expressed in care, but in the careers of its members. In greater numbers, the fallen of society and the failed within the church no longer look to the church for comfort" (The Caring Church, page 63). However, the church ought to be a community of believers who welcome wounded people and be to them a city of refuge. The loving care that they sometimes lack in general society should be available to them in the community of believers. The church ought to be like a hospital where sick and wounded individuals can get help and recover from their failures and setbacks.

The Church as a Redemptive Missionary Community

Upon reflection on the scriptures, it is evident that God's purpose is for all believers to participate in the *'Missio Dei'* (the mission of God) – in bringing his message of redemption to the peoples of the world. Ever since man sinned, God's desire and purpose has been to redeem him, and to bring him back into fellowship and communion with his God, his fellowmen, and himself as well as to restore health, and wholeness - "shalom" to every area of human life.

The mission of God incorporates a holistic ministry – involving proclamation and social action. This was demonstrated by God's deliverance of the children of Israel from Egypt's bondage. "And the Lord said: I have surely seen the oppression of my people who are in Egypt, and have heard their cry because of their taskmasters, for I know their sorrows. So, I have come down to deliver them … "(Exodus 3:7, 8a). The Lord was not only concerned about their deliverance from sin, but also from the social injustices, pain and suffering that they were experiencing. Jesus also declared, "the Spirit of the Lord is upon me, because he has anointed me to preach the gospel to the poor, he has sent me to heal the brokenhearted, to proclaim liberty to the captives and recovery of sight to the blind, to set at liberty those who are oppressed, to proclaim the acceptable year of the Lord" (Luke 4:18, 19). Jesus during his earthly ministry preached salvation from sin and ministered to the social needs of people. He promoted and practiced holistic ministry.

The medium that the Lord chose to communicate his message of grace and redemption is (primarily) through the redeemed people of God. God is oftentimes working in the world ahead of the church (Acts 10:1ff) – the Lord was communicating with Cornelius before Peter (representative of the church) got to him. Also, God is at work through leaders of government and in situations in which the church is not yet involved. "In its missionary activity, the church encounters humanity and a world in which God's salvation has already been operative, secretly, through the Spirit" (Bosch, 2002, p.). Therefore, the church at times needs to be discerning of the work of God among those to whom it takes the gospel of the kingdom and join in with what God is doing. It should join with the various social service agencies where possible to bring help to a hurtful world. However, those occurrences are exceptions to the process of how God works or continue his mission in the world. Although the Lord worked through heathen kings it seems clear that God's chosen people has been his main instrument of his deliverance in the world.

Paul emphasizing the centrality of the church (God's chosen people) as the agent of God's message of redemption in the world asked: "how then shall they call on him in whom they have not believed? And how shall they believe in him of whom they have not heard? And how shall they hear without a preacher? And how shall they preach unless they are sent? *As it is written how beautiful are the feet of those who preach the gospel of peace, who bring glad tidings of good news*" (Rom 10:14, 15). God is involved and at work in the world in places and in situations where the church is not present. However, the church is the main agent of God for fulfilling his mission in the world.

The fact that the redeemed people of God are the main medium through which God communicates his message of salvation is established very early by God through the issuing of the "*Proto evangellion*" and the subsequent call and blessing of Abraham. The Lord called Abraham and blessed him, with a view of blessing the world through him. The Lord said to Abraham, "I will make you a great nation; I will bless you and make your name great; and you shall be a blessing. I will bless those who bless you, and I will curse him who curses you; and in you all families of the earth shall be blessed" (Gen 12:2, 3). The essence of this text is that God's purpose and goal is not only to bless Abraham and his descendants, but through them to bless all the peoples of the world by bringing the message of salvation through Christ to them.

Abraham is a prototype of what every Christian is; that is, as a community of believers we are blessed to be a blessing. As the Lord blesses us, we are to reach out to the world and be God's instruments of blessing to others. Like Abraham, God has called believers and deposited his gifts and calling in them with a view of reaching the world through them.

The covenant that God made with the nation of Israel at Mount Sinai also bore out this message that God intended to bless the peoples of the world through those whom he has blessed. The Lord said to the people of Israel; "You have seen what I did to the Egyptians, and how I bore you on eagle's wings and brought you to myself. Now therefore, if you will indeed obey my voice and keep my covenant, then you shall be a special treasure to me above all people, for all the earth is mine. And you shall be to me a kingdom of priests and a holy nation" (Exod. 19:4-6a). The nation of Israel was to be a kingdom of priests before God and a holy nation. Unlike the ordained priesthood, however, their sphere of service was not in the temple, but among the nations of the world. The ordained priesthood mediates the holiness of God to the people of God, and the people of God to the peoples of the world. Thomas Dozeman in his article, "The Priestly Vocation" posited that, "It is not the ordained priests who will fulfill the vision. It is, rather, the people of God, who receive holiness through worship, empowering them upon leaving the sanctuary to become mediators of holiness to the entire world" (Dozeman, April 2005, 127).

Like the nation of Israel, the faith community is a kingdom of priest to the world: "but you are a chosen generation, a royal priesthood, a holy nation, his own special people, that you may proclaim the praises of him who call you out of darkness, into his marvelous light" (1 Pet 2:9). This advocates the priesthood of all believers. The task of winning the lost and fulfilling God's purpose in the world is not the work of a selected few, but of all the people of God.

The point that God intends that the message of redemption be taken to the peoples of the world by the people of God is further developed through the life and ministry of Jesus, and his subsequent issuing of the Great Commission. Jesus called his disciples, trained them, and commissioned them to "make disciples of all nations" (Matt 28:19). Jesus was sent into the world by the Father to fulfill the *'Missio Dei,'* and the issuing of the Great Commission by Jesus is the sending of the church into the world to continue/participate in the mission of God. John's reference to the Great Commission – "as the Father has sent me, I also send you"

(John 20:21), indicates that Jesus sends the early disciples, and by extension the church to continue the mission of God in the world – the same mission that Jesus himself was engaged in during his earthly ministry. The Great Commission therefore is the Son sending the church into the world to engage in and continue the mission of God.

The Church as a Caring Community

The church is called to be a sanctuary for those who have failed, it must be a place where such people can find help and support to overcome their setbacks in life. We sometimes expel those who have failed. However, such ought only to be the case when all attempts to facilitate reconciliation have failed, through an individual's refusal to make use of the offer of reconciliation and grace. When Adam and

Eve failed the Lord went in search for them; when the prodigal son "run" back to his father, the father welcomed him with open arms.

God's forgiveness flows from his heart of love and compassion for fallen humanity. Although the sinner deserves punishment ("the wages of sin is death" Romans 6:23), God acts graciously and forgive the wrongdoer of his wrongdoing. "For God so loved the world the world that he gave his begotten Son, that whoever believes in him should have everlasting life. For God did not send his Son into the world to condemn the world, but that the world through him might be saved" (John 3:16, 17). "For scarcely for a righteous man will one die; yet perhaps for a good man someone would even dare to die. But God demonstrates his own love toward us, in that while we were still sinners, Christ died for us" (Romans 5:7, 8). Once the sinner acknowledges his sin and seek forgiveness from the Lord will forgive. For "if we confess our sins, He is faithful and just to forgive us our sins and to cleanse us from all unrighteousness" (I John 1:9).

God's forgiveness is grounded in the sacrificial death of Christ. Christ's death is an atoning sacrifice; he died for us and is the means by which our sins are forgiven, and us being reconciled to God.

"For Christ also suffered once for sins, the just for the unjust, that he might bring us to God, being put to death in the flesh but made alive by the Spirit" (I Peter 3:18);" for he made him who knew no sin to be sin for us, that we might become the righteousness of God in him" (2 Corinthians 5:21; see also Romans 5:10; Galatians 1:4; Ephesians 5:2; Hebrews 9:28). Because of Christ death, God can forgive the sins of fallen humanity. Those who believe in Christ Jesus no longer bear the ultimate consequence for their sins – "there is therefore now no condemnation to those who are in Christ Jesus" (Romans 8:1). Through Christ's death, God can forgive the sinner and be both just and the justifier (Romans 3:26).

When the Lord forgives an individual, he removes his sins as far as the east from the west from the individual and wipes his slate clean. This aspect of the divine forgiveness is expressed through the words of the prophets among other scripture references – "As far as the east is from the west, so far has he removed our transgressions from us" (Psalm 103:12); "You have cast all my sins behind your back" (Isaiah 38:17); "I, even I, am he who blots out your transgressions for my own sake; and I will not remember your sins" (Isaiah 43:25); "for I will forgive their iniquity, and their sin I will remember no more" (Jeremiah 31:34); "You will cast all our sins into the depths of the sea" (Micah 7:19). In divine forgiveness our sins are expunged if you will. God sees the individual who he forgives as if he has never sinned.

Another important aspect of forgiveness is its relationship to reconciliation. Forgiveness and reconciliation are both acts of divine grace and are given as gifts based on Christ's death. In forgiveness God graciously cancels the debt owed my man on account of his sins. While in reconciliation, God makes provision and invites sinful man to share friendship and fellowship with him. However, "Forgiveness is not the equivalent of reconciliation, however, it is the means by which barriers to reconciliation (which may or may not follow) are removed" (Dict. of Pastoral Care and Counseling, page 438).

There is also a connection between divine forgiveness and restoration. Divine forgiveness signifies that despite humanity's sin and imperfections they can be forgiven and restored through God's grace. Restoration can be viewed as the process through which individuals are renewed, both spiritually and morally, following their acceptance of divine forgiveness. God promised to renew and restore Israel: "I will give you a new heart and put a new spirit within you; I will take the heart of stone out of your flesh and give you a heart of flesh. I will put my Spirit within you and cause you to walk in my statutes, and you will keep my judgments and do them" (Ezekiel 36:26, 27). God's promised restoration is also expressed in the message of Joel 2:25 – "So I will restore to you the years that the swarming locust has eaten, the crawling locust, the consuming locust, and the chewing locust."

CITY OF REFUGE – THE CHURCH AS A CITY OF REFUGE

Divine forgiveness, reconciliation and restoration is beautifully illustrated in Jesus' parable of the Prodigal Son, or more so the parable of the compassionate father (Luke 15:11-32). In the parable, the son took his inheritance, went into a far country, and spent his inheritance on reckless living. However, when he came to himself, he decided to return home to his father. "But when he was still a great way off, his father saw him and had compassion, and ran and fell on his neck and kissed him." The father said to his servants, "Bring out the best robe and put it on him and put a ring on his hand and sandals on his feet. And bring the fatted calf here and kill it and let us eat and be merry; for this my son was dead and is alive again; he was lost and is found." (Luke 15:20-24). The prodigal son was not only forgiven by his father, but he was also restored. This parable illustrates God's love and eagerness to forgive and restore those who turn to him in repentance.

The church's attitude toward forgiveness and restoration should follow or be reflective of the nature God's forgiveness and restoration. Today's church does extend forgiveness to those who have failed the church, and it does call those who are outside of the church to repent of their sins and accept God's offer forgiveness and reconciliation. However, the church at times does not go all the way in displaying all the elements of God's forgiveness. Whereas in God's forgiveness the repented sinner's sin is forgotten, and he is no more judged according to his past sin. He is accepted as a bone fide member of the body of Christ; he is renewed and restored. The church at times continue to withhold certain privileges for service and like in the wider society the sinner's pass record of sin is not removed as is the case with God's forgiveness. Following the divine example, the church should expunge the record of failures when such individuals have repented and gone through the process to have such records expunged – submission to church discipline and counseling, etc., and have demonstrated credible signs that they have changed from their previous sinful behaviors.

The church should not seek perfection for involvement in the ministry of the church. The Lord calls and commissions us, knowing fully well that we have flaws and shortcomings. Since God himself, has committed the fulfillment of his will into the hands of imperfect human beings, the church should not be afraid to engage persons whom God has called and cleansed (though imperfect) from engaging in ministry.

The church does provide a place for counseling and restoration for those who have failed, but like the wider society, when those who have paid for the failures returned to society they are treated as second class citizens; the church treats the restored as second-class members by restricting them from functioning in certain areas of the church ministries. This approach has no biblical support and is rather a result of the impact of our culture. The church must make greater provision to facilitate the return to normal functioning when persons have showed evidence of transformation and restoration. It must find ways to reduce and ultimately remove the stigma from those who have repented of wrong doings and demonstrated evidence of transformation and restoration.

The Church and the Law of The Land

The church should use whatever available means it has to lobby for reform in the legal system that provide hope for those who have failed and have paid their dues to society for their crimes to have their criminal records expunged and create a roadmap for such individuals to be reassimilated into the general society. It should lobby the courts to develop a system that provides easy access to and broadens the eligibility for the expungement of criminal records. An integral part of such a system could be that the church or some agencies be adequately equipped to inform and educate convicts who have served their time the options that are available when they meet the requirements for having their records obliterated.

Likewise, in accordance with the principles of the "City of Refuge" the church should also make room for those of its members who have failed to properly reintegrate into the life and ministries of the church, when these members and leaders have repented of their sins and demonstrate credible signs that they have changed. If the church is to be true to its nature, it should not seek perfection for involvement in the ministries of the church. Failure does not nullify usefulness in the life of the church, neither does it nullify the call to the ministry. Since God himself, has committed the fulfillment of his plan into the hands of imperfect and frail human beings (2 Corinthians 4:7, see also I Corinthians 1:26-29); the church should not be afraid to engage persons whom God has called and cleansed from engaging in ministry. To do does not mean the church has compromised its values and its stand on holiness to be God's standard of living for his people. Instead, the church is remaining true to its nature as a place where wounded people, who, through their weaknesses and susceptibility to failures have failed can find a safe place to be restored and replenished – a "City of Refuge". By being welcoming and compassionate to those who have failed on their journey of life; by being that place where individuals who have been rejected by the wider society can gain a second chance; by making the rehabilitation of those whom society has neglected, because of their faults and failures a prominent area of ministry – a "City of Refuge".

Jesus in the parable of the great supper said the master commanded his servants saying. "Go out quickly into the streets and lanes of the city and bring in here the poor and the maimed and the lame and the blind" (Luke 14:21b). What the city of refuge is to the man slayer who accidentally and unintentionally kill someone, the church is to the those who have failed on their journey of life. It can serve as a model for the rest of society as to how people who have failed should be treated.

THE CITY OF REFUGE

The man slayer may return to the wider society after the death of the high priest. Through this medium, the Lord through divine providence determines when the manslayer is fit and ready for the wider society. The church, which as God's representative here on earth (give biblical support) functions in a similar role to determine when those in the city of refuge are ready to return to the wider society. The church can discern when transformation has taken place. While the church may not be able to judge those who are outside the city of refuge, the church is able to judge those inside. One may argue that we cannot be sure that there will not be a relapse of those who have fled for refuge in the city of refuge.

CHAPTER 6

RECOMMENDATIONS

The church as God's instrument of blessing to the world, has the responsibility to respond to the sufferings in the world as our Lord Jesus taught and practice during his earthly ministry. H. Richard Niebuhr in his essay on *"The Responsibility of the Church for Society,"* stated that, "The church looks not only to the absolute in the finite but to the redemptive principle in the absolute. God, it believes and confesses, is love; He is mercy; He so loved the world that he gave His best-loved for its redemption; it is his will that the wicked should not perish but turn from their ways and live. To be a Christian church is to be a community which is always aware of and always responding to the redemptive principle in the world, to Christ-in-God, to the Redeemer" (https://www.religion-online.org/article/the-responsibility-of-the-church-for-society).

The church can develop an approach to ministry that promotes liberation, empowerment, and transformation (LET). Those who respond to the gospel and come to the church can experience liberation from sin and the effects of sin, be empowered to access available resources to improve their lives and be transformed to the point where they become actively involved in liberation, empowerment, and transformation (LET) of others.

THE CITY OF REFUGE

Creating a church environment that serves as a "city of refuge" for individuals who are suffering due to past failures and shortcomings requires a compassionate and welcoming community.

The following are some recommendations on how a church and other organizations that are so inclined can become more involved in this important mission. Local assemblies can adopt and implement those that they are equipped to manage.

- Speak openly where practical against the social ills of society, while being the embodiment of what ought to be the correct and appropriate response to the conditions. The church has a responsibility to use the platforms that are available to stand up and speak up for what is right and not remain silent. It must become the voice of "poor."
- Practice an approach to ministry which is expressed through proclamation of the word and social action - word and deed.
- Creating an atmosphere that is conducive to self-disclosure, so that those who have failed may come clean and experience healing. Such a place would provide hope (that is more than mere words) for those who have submitted to the discipline and have demonstrated evidence of transformation; and being welcoming and compassionate to those who have failed on their journey of life. Such a place that acts redemptively toward those that fall short of acceptable standards.
- Practice an approach to ministry that makes rehabilitation of those whom society reject and neglect (the 'poor') because of their faults and failure a prominent area of ministry.
- Emphasize the biblical teachings of forgiveness, redemption, and second chances. These concepts are central to the Christian faith and are essential for spiritual healing and renewal. The church is that place - "city of refuge," where individuals who have failed can experience spiritual healing, renewal, and restoration.

RECOMMENDATIONS

- Cultivate a non-judgmental and accepting atmosphere within the church community. Ensure that individuals who have made mistakes or experience failures feel safe and supportive in sharing their struggles and stories without fear of judgment and condemnation. This can be achieved by creating small groups or support groups where individuals can share their experiences and receive encouragement.
- Create support groups of recovery ministries for specific issues such as addiction, divorce, grief, or mental health challenges. These groups can provide a sense of belonging and understanding for those struggling.
- The church should promote accountability among its members by encouraging them to take responsibility for their actions and seek help when needed. This can be done by creating accountability groups or partnering with organizations that provide accountability services.
- Offer pastoral counseling services and/or refer individuals to professional counselors who can provide guidance and support for unique challenges.
- Educate the congregation about the struggles people face, including the stigma associated with certain issues.
- Encourage empathy and understanding among church members. Empathy is a key component in communicating love and care for one another. To develop this all-important quality there is the need to encourage and practice active listening, read books and articles and other literature that explore different perspectives, encourage volunteering for cause that the church care about, and make use of professionals - therapists and counselors as the need for such services arise. Doing bible studies on the 'one another' passages in the bible is also of utmost important in the development of empathy – cognitive empathy, emotional empathy, and compassionate empathy.

- Establish a prayer ministry dedicated to interceding for individuals who are suffering. Encourage congregants to pray for those in need and to share their prayer requests.
- Extend warm and welcoming hospitality to newcomers and returning members. Greet them with open arms and a genuine interest in their well-being.
- Implement mentorship programs where experienced members can offer guidance and support to those who are struggling spiritually and otherwise. Individuals can be paired with mentors who have gone through similar experiences and can provide guidance and support. Where mentors with such experiences are not available in a local assembly, referrals can be made.
- Engage in community outreach programs that address social issues, and partner with local organizations – nonprofits, charities, or other groups that provide resources and support for those in need. The church can also work with probation officers and law enforcement agencies in the rehabilitation of individuals with criminal records; it can sponsor events that address social issues such as poverty, homelessness, or addiction. By partnering with these organizations, the church can leverage their resources and expertise to make a positive impact in the community.
- Share success stories of individuals who have overcome their past failures and shortcomings through faith and support from the church. Celebrate their transformations as a source of inspiration.
- Provide practical assistance such as food banks, clothing drives, or financial counseling to individuals facing economic challenges.
- Ensure that worship services are inclusive and relevant to people from all walks of life. Messages should resonate with those who have experienced hardship and failures while

RECOMMENDATIONS

remaining true to biblical truths – they should promote grace and truth together.

- Offer workshops and seminars on personal development, life skills, and financial literacy to empower individuals to make positive changes in their lives. These workshops and seminars should include such topics as communication skills, conflict resolution, time management, stress management, budgeting, investing and debt management. Personal development workshops will help individuals identify their strengths and weaknesses, set goals, and develop strategies for personal growth. By providing valuable information and resources that can help people develop new skills, the church can play a significant role in helping those who have failed on their journey of life find hope and healing.
- Recognize that the journey to recovery and healing is often long-term. Continue to offer support and encouragement even after initial crises have passed.
- Organize community building events and activities that foster a sense of belonging and friendship among members. Community events facilitate social connections which can be a crucial source of support. By fostering social connections and providing opportunities for people to connect with one another, the church can help build stronger communities and promote positive change.
- Encourage open conversations about mental health and emotional struggles within the church community. Break down the stigma surrounding these issues. Encouraging open conversation about mental health helps create a safe and supportive environment where people feel comfortable sharing their struggles. This can be done by providing resources such as support groups, counseling services, and educational materials that help people understand mental health issues and how to cope with them.

- Set an example of humility and transparency within the church leadership. Leaders who acknowledge their own imperfections can create a culture of authenticity.

These recommendations are by no means exhaustive, much more work needs to be done, especially in involving individuals who have committed grievous crimes such as child abuse before they are fully incorporated in the children's ministry and the like. Creating a "city of refuge" within the church is an ongoing process that requires dedication and a commitment to love, support and serve those who are suffering. By implementing these recommendations, church can become a beacon of hope and healing for individuals seeking redemption and a fresh start.

REFERENCES

Blosch, David J. *Transforming Mission: Paradigm Shifts in Theology of Mission*. New York: Orbis Books, Maryknoll, 2002.

Boice, James Montgomery. *Joshua: An Expositional Commentary*. Grand Rapids, Michigan: Baker Books, 2006.

Greenberg, Moshe. "The Biblical Conception of Asylum," *Journal of Biblical Literature 1* (June 1959): 125-132.

Murphy, James G. *Critical and Exegetical Commentary on The Book Exodus, With new Translation*. Boston: W.H. Halliday and Company, 1868.

Pennsylvania General Assembly. www.legis.state.pa.us/cfdocs/legisll/uconsCheck.cfm?yr=2018&sesslnd=0&act=56.

Prin, John Howard. *Secret Keeping: Overcoming Hidden habits and Addictions*. Navato, California: New World Library, 2006.

Rhea, Homer G., ed. *Preaching The Word Today*. Cleveland Tennessee: Pathway Press, 2002.

Sakenfeld, Katharine Doob, General ed. *The New Interpreter's Dictionary of the Bible, Vol. 1*. Nashville, Tennessee: Abingdon Press, 2006.

Silvoso, Ed. *Prayer Evangelism*. Bloomington, Minnesota: Chosen Books, 2000.

Stott, John R.W. *The Message of Romans.* Leicester, England: Inter-Varsity Press, 1994.

The Responsibility of the Church for Society. https://www.religion-Online.org/article/the-responsibility-of-the-church-for-Society/

Unger, Merrill F. *The New Unger's Bible Dictionary.* Chicago: The Moody Bible Institute of Chicago, 2005.

Printed in the USA
CPSIA information can be obtained
at www.ICGtesting.com
LVHW091735300124
770329LV00002B/226